OSPREY PUBLISHING CLASSIC BATTLES MILITARY BOOK CLUB

SAIPAN & TINIAN 1944

PIERCING THE JAPANESE EMPIRE

CLASSIC BATTLES

OSPREY PUBLISHING

SAIPAN & TINIAN 1944
PIERCING THE JAPANESE EMPIRE

GORDON L ROTTMAN

ISBN 1 84176 861 8

Editor: Lee Johnson
Design: The Black Spot
Index by David Worthington
Maps by The Map Studio
3D bird's-eye views by John Plumer
Battlescene artwork by Howard Gerrard
Originated by The Electronic Page Company, Cwmbran, UK
Printed in China through World Print Ltd.

04 05 06 07 08   10 9 8 7 6 5 4 3 2 1

For a catalog of all books published by Osprey Military
and Aviation please contact:

Osprey Direct USA, c/o MBI Publishing, P.O. Box 1,
729 Prospect Ave, Osceola, WI 54020, USA
E-mail: info@ospreydirectusa.com

Osprey Direct UK, P.O. Box 140, Wellingborough,
Northants, NN8 2FA, UK
E-mail: info@ospreydirect.co.uk

www.ospreypublishing.com

Artist's note

KEY TO MILITARY SYMBOLS

ARMY GROUP · ARMY · CORPS · DIVISION · BRIGADE
REGIMENT · BATTALION · COMPANY · INFANTRY · CAVALRY
ARTILLERY · ARMOUR · MOTORIZED · AIRBORNE · SPECIAL FORCES

Author's Note

Abbreviations

AAA	anti-aircraft artillery
Adm	Admiral
amtrac	amphibian tractor (see also LVT)
AT	anti-tank
BAR	Browning automatic rifle
CINCPOA	Commander in Chief, Pacific Ocean Area
CO	Commanding Officer
CP	Command Post
CT	Combat Team (2nd MarDiv)
DUKW	2½-ton amphibious truck ("Duck")
FMF	Fleet Marine Force
HQ	Headquarters
IIIAC	III Amphibious Corps
IIB	Independent Infantry Battalion (IJA)
IMB	Independent Mixed Brigade (IJA)
IGHQ	Imperial General Headquarters
InfDiv	Infantry Division (US Army)
IJA	Imperial Japanese Army
IJN	Imperial Japanese Navy
LCI	Landing Craft, Infantry
LCM	Landing Craft, Mechanized
LCT	Landing Craft, Tank
LCVP	Landing Craft, Vehicle and Personnel
LFBL	Landing Force Beachhead Line
LSD	Landing Ship, Dock
LST	Landing Ship, Tank
LVT	Landing Vehicle, Tracked ("amtrac")
LVT(A)	Landing Vehicle, Tracked (Armored)
MarBde	Marine Brigade
MarDiv	Marine Division
MP	Military Police
NC	Naval Construction (battalion) ("Seabees")
NCO	non-commissioned officer
NTLF	Northern Troops and Landing Force
O-1	Objective 1 Line (first day's objective)
Prov	Provisional (temporary unit)
RCT	Regimental Combat Team (4th Marine and 27th InfDiv)
SNLF	Special Naval Landing Force (Japanese)
STLF	Southern Troops and Landing Force
TF	Task Force
TG	Task Group
UDT	Underwater Demolition Team
US	United States
USA	United States Army
USMC	United States Marine Corps
VAC	V Amphibious Corps
(-)	reduced (elements detached from parent unit)
(+)	reinforced (additional elements attached)

Comparative ranks

US Marine and Army Officers	Japanese Army Officers
2ndLt: 2nd Lieutenant	SubLt: Sub-Lieutenant
1stLt: 1st Lieutenant	Lt: Lieutenant
Capt: Captain	Capt: Captain
Maj: Major	Maj: Major
LtCol: Lieutenant Colonel	LtCol: Lieutenant Colonel
Col: Colonel	Col: Colonel
BGen: Brigadier General ("one-star")	MajGen: Major General
MajGen: Major General ("two-star")	LtGen: Lieutenant General
LtGen: Lieutenant General ("three-star")	—
Gen: General ("four-star")	Gen: General

Battalions organic to US Marine and Army regiments are designated with the
battalion and regimental number, e.g. 1/6 is 1st Bn., 6th Marines and 2/165 is
2nd Bn., 165th Infantry Regiment. Companies and batteries are designated in a
similar manner, e.g. B/1/6 – Company B, 1st Battalion, 6th Marines. Japanese
battalions are similarly designated; e.g., II/135 is II Bn., 135th Regiment.
The Japanese place the surname first and the personal name second.
Contemporary and post-war writings usually reverse the two. This book follows
the Japanese practice.

Editor's note

Readers should consult Campaign 139 *Guam 1941 & 1944* for maps of the
strategic situation in the Pacific Theater at the end of 1943 and Japanese
deployments in the Mariana Islands in the Summer of 1944.

Page 2 The 105th Infantry coming ashore on the "Yellow" Beaches on J+2.

CONTENTS

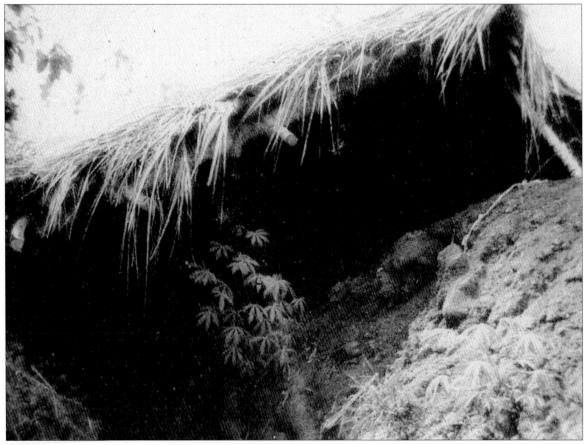

INTRODUCTION

By the summer of 1944 the Allied counteroffensive in the Pacific was in full swing. The Solomon and Bismarck Islands in the South Pacific had long been secured, as had eastern New Guinea by General Douglas MacArthur's Southwest Pacific forces. In the Central Pacific, the Gilbert Islands had been cleared the previous year and the Marshalls had been seized. Some bypassed Japanese garrisons remained in these areas, but they were slowly being bombed and starved into submission and posed no threat. The great Japanese naval and air bases at Rabaul on New Britain and Truk in the Marshalls had been neutralized, giving the US Third and Fifth Fleets free rein in the Central Pacific. In September 1943, the *Imperial General Headquarters* (IGHQ) established Japan's outer defense line running from the Dutch East Indies, through eastern New Guinea, the Carolines, Marshalls, and Marianas. However, the thrust into the Marshalls had already penetrated this line. Beginning in April–May 1944 the Allies conducted several landings on the north coast of New Guinea. In the Central Pacific, the Marianas would be the next Allied objective.

ORIGINS OF THE CAMPAIGN

Long-range planning for the Pacific War was directed through a series of high-level conferences between the US president, the British prime minister, occasionally other heads of state, and the chiefs of staff of the combined armed forces. The January 1943 Casablanca Conference, while establishing basic objectives for the war in the Pacific, did not include the Mariana Islands among them. The same applied to the May "Trident" Conference. Objectives in the Central Pacific were expanded, but still the Marianas were not specifically included. At both conferences the Navy had argued the importance of seizing the Marianas making full use of its growing fleets, both for liberating the Philippines and for the invasion of Japan, but this was ignored. At the same time General MacArthur remained totally focused on this Southwest Pacific drive with the objective of seizing the Philippines via New Guinea. He opposed a major thrust through the Central Pacific fearing that it would siphon resources from his efforts. Ironically, it would be one of the Navy's strongest opponents that ultimately urged that the road to Tokyo should be driven through the Central Pacific. The Air Force's new long-range bomber, the B-29, was now being deployed. The only operating bases within range of Japan were in China. This forced the Superfortresses to fly to their maximum range and still allowed them to reach targets in only parts of Japan. The logistics of transporting ordnance, fuel, spare parts, and all the other necessary supplies into China from India was a major difficulty. The Air

This machine-gun position was constructed of limestone rocks, blended into the surrounding terrain, and well camouflaged with brush. Most of the flamethrower-scorched brush had been pulled away to reveal the position. Such positions were well camouflaged and too small for naval gunfire spotters to detect and had to be reduced by infantrymen.

Force pointed out that airbases in the Marianas would place Japan within the bombers' range and could be easily supplied by ships direct from the United States. With the Navy and Air Force joining forces at the December 1943 Cairo Conference ("Sextant"), they successfully argued that a two-prong attack through the Central Pacific and the Philippines would more effectivcly achieve the defeat of Japan. This would secure objectives from which they could conduct intensive air bombardment and establish a sea and air blockade against Japan, and from which an invasion of Japan proper could be launched if necessary. The Central Pacific Operation Plan, "Granite II", was completed on 27 December 1943 with a tentative date for seizing Saipan, Tinian, and Guam of 15 November 1944.

In war, plans change once a campaign is under way and "Granite" was no exception. It was kicked off exactly on schedule with the 31 January 1944 assault on Kwajalein in the Marshalls. The speedy success of this operation freed reserves to seize Eniwetok two months early, in February rather than May. At the same time MacArthur again attempted to sell his plan and even convinced some on Admiral Chester Nimitz's Pacific Fleet staff that the New Guinea and Philippine route was more favorable and that a drive through the Central Pacific was unnecessary. When presented to Admiral Ernest King, Chief of Naval Operations, he chastised Nimitz for failing to stay the course. The Marianas assault was moved forward two weeks. In mid-February the formidable Imperial Japanese Navy (IJN) bastion at Truk in the central Marshalls, the "Gibraltar of the Pacific," was neutralized by sea and air. This suddenly opened the way to the Marianas. MacArthur too was able to step up his operations and quickly seized the Admiralty Islands at the end of February. The Washington Planning Conference in February and March 1944 set the schedule for the remainder of the Pacific War. Of the six phases identified by the Joint Chiefs of Staff, number 4 was, "Establishment of control of the Marianas–Carolines–Palau area by Nimitz's forces by neutralizing Truk; by occupying the southern Marianas, target date 15 June 1944; and by occupying the Palaus, target date 15 September 1944."

Seizing only Guam would have both satisfied the political need to expunge the US defeat in 1941 and provided a base for the airfields from which to bomb Japan. Saipan and Tinian could have been neutralized by naval and air power. However, it was thought better to destroy the significant enemy forces on these islands and to develop airbases on the more favorable terrain. In addition Saipan and Tinian were 100 miles (161km) closer to Japan than Guam.

To support operational planning, up-to-date intelligence was required. Navy aircraft took the first aerial photos of Saipan and Tinian in February, but clouds prevented full coverage. Additional missions in April filled the gaps. Photo update missions were flown in May. In April a submarine photographed the shorelines of both islands, but no reconnaissance teams attempted to infiltrate the island.

THE MARIANA ISLANDS

The Mariana Islands chain ("Gateway") is known to the Japanese as Mariana Shoto. The Marianas' 15 islands run north to south in a shallow curving chain 425 miles (684km) long, some 300 miles (483km) due north of the West Caroline Islands. Pearl Harbor is 3,400 miles (5,471km) to the east, Tokyo 1,260 miles (2,028km) to the north-northwest, and Manila 1,500 miles (2,414km) to the west. Some 500 miles (805km) to the northwest is Iwo Jima, the next stepping-stone to Tokyo.

Direct US involvement with the islands began on 21 June 1898, during the Spanish–American War, when the cruiser USS *Charleston* landed a Marine detachment on Guam and accepted the governor's surrender. The island was soon a US possession. In 1899 the remainder of the Marianas, Marshalls, and Carolines were purchased from Spain by Germany. In October 1914, after the beginning of World War I, the Japanese seized the islands.

In December 1920 Japan was granted a mandate by the League of Nations to govern the former German possessions, effective 1 April 1922. In December 1914 the Japanese established the "South Seas Defense Force" to garrison what became known simply as the Japanese Mandate. In 1935 Japan declared the Mandate closed to Westerners after serving its mandatory two-year notice to the League of Nations, from which it withdrew. It was not long before the popular press began referring to the Mandate as "Japan's islands of mystery."

Japan activated the 4th Fleet on 15 November 1939 to defend the Mandate with amphibious and light forces. Each of the three main island groups was provided with an independent defense system centered on Jaluit, Truk, and Saipan. The defense strategy was to marshal, service, and supply 4th Fleet air and naval forces as they launched raids and small-scale operations out of range of Allied bases and reconnaissance aircraft. This would buy time as the Combined Fleet sortied to meet the approaching US fleet and defeat it in the long-desired decisive engagement.

Saipan

Saipan ("Tattersalls") is the second largest island in the Marianas measuring $12^{1}/_{2}$ miles (20km) from northeast to southwest and $5^{1}/_{2}$ miles (8.9km) across the center. It covers 85 square miles. Saipan is 100 miles (161km) north-northeast of Guam.

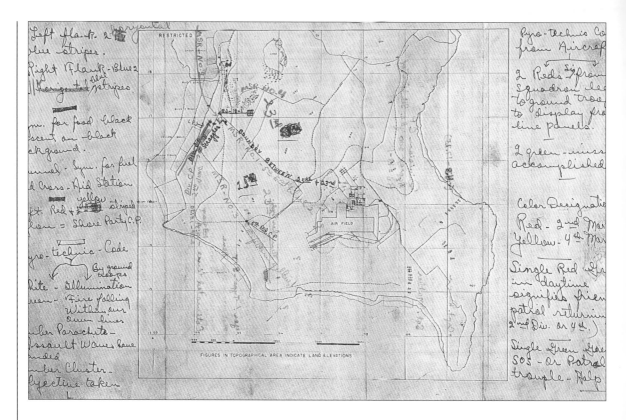

Much of Saipan's 54-mile (87km) coastline is faced with cliffs of varying height providing only 14 miles (22.5km) of beaches. A coral barrier reef fringes much of the island, with a submerged arm curving out from the upper west coast to enclose Tanapag harbor. Tiny Maniagassa Island lies near the harbor's entrance. Projecting from the southeast corner of the island is Nafutan Peninsula and 4,000yds (3,640m) north across Magicienne Bay is Kagman Peninsula. The bay's shore is faced by broken, cave-riddled cliffs and fringed with coral outcroppings and a reef.

A rolling plateau 200–300ft (61–91m) above sea level covers the southern third of the island. Marsh-rimmed Lake Susupe was located 3/4 mile (1.2km) inland from Afetna Point. The island's center is dominated by 1,554ft (474m) Mount Tapotchau rising from the north edge of the southern plateau in a series of terraced ridges. Just to its southwest is the second highest feature, 1,133ft (345m) Mount Tipo Pale. A rugged 400–934ft (122–285m) ridgeline runs 7 miles (11.3km) north to Mount Marpi (833ft/254m), located near the island's north end. Approximately 70 per cent of Saipan was covered with sugarcane. Low scrub trees, brush, and high, dense grasses covered the hilly areas.

Garapan is the largest town and the administrative center of the Marianas. Just to the southeast was the radio station. South of Afetna Point and Susupe Lake is the island's second largest town, Charan Kanoa, and its sugar refinery. Tanapag is near Tanapag Harbor's north side and was the third largest town. Numerous concrete and masonry buildings were found in the larger towns, but most commercial buildings and dwellings were of wood-frame construction. Both types of buildings had corrugated sheet metal roofs. A few small villages were scattered about the island. All towns were utterly destroyed in the fighting.

Marine sketch map of southern Saipan issued to 4th MarDiv troops for pre-landing orientation – Not to be Taken Ashore.

The island's 4,500ft-long (1,365m) Aslito Airfield (also known as Isloto) is located on the plain at the base of the Nafutan Peninsula on the south end. It was built in 1934 to be the first in the Marianas. The Charan Kanoa (also known as Oreai to the Japanese) emergency landing strip (3,875ft/1,175m long) was located to the north of Charan Kanoa just behind the "Green" Beaches and another airstrip was located on the island's north end at Marpi Point. Both were begun in 1944, but never completed. A seaplane base, built in 1935, was located at Flores Point on the north edge of Tanapag Harbor. Not even minimal coast defense installations were built on Saipan until 1940–41.

Rota and Pagan, the two other islands occupied by the Japanese, were not assaulted. They were periodically bombed from June and surrendered on 2 September 1945.

Tinian

Tinian Island ("Tearaway") is 3 miles (3.2km) south of Saipan separated by the Saipan Straits. Guam is some 85 miles (137km) to the south-southwest. Five miles (8km) south of Tinian is small, uninhabited Aguijan Island.

Most of the island consists of an approximately 200ft (61m) plateau. It is 10^1/$_4$ miles (16.5km) from the northern Ushi Point to the southern Lalo Point and 5 miles (8km) at it widest across the center. While mostly flat, there are two hills near the northwest end, 390ft (118m) Mount Maga and just to its southeast 564ft (172m) Mount Lasso. About 90 percent of the island consisted of cultivated square or rectangular farm plots of sugarcane, bordered by small irrigation ditches or windbreaks of trees and hedgerows. Hilly ground was covered with low scrub trees and dense brush. The cane fields were crisscrossed with a grid of one-lane dirt roads. A narrow-gauge railroad for hauling cane to the refineries ran out of Tinian Town with spurs to the southeast, west, and north. The four airfields were 4,700ft-long (1,433m) Nos. 1 and 3 near the north end at Ushi Point, No. 2 (5,000ft/1524m long) on the east coast at Gurguan Point, and uncompleted No. 4 northwest of Tinian Town. On Suharon Bay on the southwest coast was the only town, Tinian Town. Located there were two sugar mills and port facilities.

CHRONOLOGY

1944

30 January–23 February US Marines and Army secure the Marshall Islands.

17–18 February US Navy neutralizes Japanese air and naval base at Truk.

22–23 February US Navy conducts attacks in southern Marianas.

29 February US Army assaults Admiralty Islands.

12 March Joint Chiefs of Staff direct that southern Marianas be seized.

20 March US Marines secure Emirau. US Navy establishes objectives of the Marianas operation.

22 March US Army assaults Hollandia, New Guinea.

23 March Pacific Fleet issues Marianas operation order.

12 April V Amphibious Corps (VAC) staff split to form Expeditionary Troops and Northern Troops and Landing Force (NTLF) staffs.

23 April Pacific Fleet issues operation plan.

26 April Expeditionary Troops issues operation plan.

27 April NTLF issues initial operation plan.

1 May NTLF issues revised operation plan.

17–19 May NTLF conducts rehearsals in Hawaii.

Late May 43rd Division and 47th Independent Mixed Brigade (IMB) arrive on Saipan.

25 May Lead elements, Landing Ships, Tank (LST), of Joint Expeditionary Force departs Hawaii for Eniwetok.

29–30 May Troop transports depart Hawaii for Eniwetok.

6–11 June Joint Expeditionary Force assembles at Eniwetok.

11–13 June Preparatory naval and air bombardment of Saipan, Tinian, and Guam commences as do air attacks on Rota and Pagan Islands.

14 June Northern and Southern Attack Forces commence bombardment of Saipan. Demonstration conducted off Saipan's northwest coast.

15 June (D-Day) 2nd and 4th MarDivs land on Saipan.

16 June First aircraft land on Charan Kanoa Airstrip. Bombardment of Guam commences.

16–20 June 27th InfDiv lands on Saipan.

Night 16/17 June Japanese launch counterattack and are defeated.

16–17 June XXIV Corps Artillery lands.

18 June Saipan's east coast reached. Aslito Airfield seized.

19–20 June Battle of the Philippine Sea.

20 June After clearing the south, 4th MarDiv attacks north with 2nd MarDiv. Shelling of Tinian from Saipan commences.

21 June Aslito Airfield operational for fighters.

22 June 27th InfDiv takes up position between 2nd and 4th MarDivs and the push into central Saipan begins.

24 June Commanding general, 27th InfDiv relieved by LtGen Smith and MajGen Jarman assumes command.

25 June Mt. Tapotchau and Kagman Peninsula seized.

26 June Shelling and bombardment of Tinian increases. Emperor Hirohito requests that Foreign Minister seek peace settlement.

28 June MajGen Grimes assumes command of 27th InfDiv.

30 June 2nd MarDiv pinched out of line.

3 July Garapan seized.

4 July Tanapag Seaplane Base secured.

6/7 July Final mass *banzai* charge defeated on Tanapag Plain. 27th InfDiv pinched out of line.

7 July Command of Japanese Tinian forces transferred from Northern Marianas Army Group on Saipan to Southern Marianas Army Group on Guam.

OPERATION CALENDAR	
Saipan	
D-Day	15 June
D+1	16 June
D+2	17 June
D+3	18 June
D+4	19 June
D+5	20 June
D+6	21 June
D+7	22 June
D+8	23 June
D+9	24 June
D+10	25 June
D+11	26 June
D+12	27 June
D+13	28 June
D+14	29 June
D+15	30 June
D+16	1 July
D+17	2 July
D+18	3 July
D+19	4 July
D+20	5 July
D+21	6 July
D+22	7 July
D+23	8 July
D+24	9 July
Battle of the Philippine Sea	
D+4–D+5	19-20 June
Tinian	
J-Day	24 July
J+1	25 July
J+2	26 July
J+3	27 July
J+4	28 July
J+5	29 July
J+6	30 July
J+7	31 July
J+8	1 August
Guam	
W-Day	21 July
W+19	9 August (secured)

9 July 4th MarDiv reaches Marpi Point and Saipan is declared secure.

10 July 4th and 2nd MarDivs begin preparations for Tinian landing.

10/11 July "White" Beaches on Tinian are reconnoitered.

12 July MajGen Schmidt assumes command of VAC/NTLF to allow LtGen Smith to oversee Guam operation. MajGen Cates assumes command of 4th MarDiv. Garrison Command assumes control of Saipan.

13 July Maniagassa Island in Tanapag Harbor seized. NTLF issues operation order for Tinian assault.

16 July Japanese Government announces Saipan's fall.

18 July Prime Minister Tojo and cabinet forced to resign.

20 July 4th and 2nd MarDivs begin embarkation for Tinian.

21 July (W-Day) 3rd MarDiv and 1st Provisional MarBde land on Guam.

23 July 4th and 2nd MarDivs depart Saipan for Tinian.

23–24 July 77th InfDiv lands on Guam.

24 Jul (J-Day) 4th MarDiv lands on Tinian.

25 July 2nd MarDiv lands on Tinian. Tanapag Harbor on Saipan reopened.

27 July XXIV Corps Artillery begins relocating to Tinian. Ushi Point Airfield becomes operational.

31 July Final Japanese counterattack on Tinian.

1 August Tinian declared secure.

9 August Aslito Airfield operational for B-24 bombers.

10 August Guam declared secure. NTLF dissolved and VAC resumes normal duties. Island Command assumes control of Tinian.

12 August Commander, Forward Area relieves Commander, Joint Expeditionary Force of responsibility for Saipan and Tinian.

1 September Naval Operating Base, Saipan commissioned.

15 October Aslito Airfield operational for B-29 bombers.

24 November Saipan-based B-29s bomb Tokyo.

30 December First B-29s land on Tinian.

1945

4 February Tinian-based B-29s bomb Kobe.

6 August Atomic bomb dropped on Hiroshima.

9 August Atomic bomb dropped on Nagasaki.

10 August Japan sues for peace.

14 August Ceasefire in Pacific Theater.

2 September Japan formally surrenders (V-J Day). Japanese forces on Rota and Pagan surrender.

POST-WAR

2 January 1947 Trust Territory of the Pacific Islands established by UN.

1 June 1947 Naval Base, Tinian decommissioned.

30 June 1949 Navy Operating Base, Saipan decommissioned.

30 June 1951 Naval administration ceases and Department of the Interior authority commences.

4 November 1986 Commonwealth of the Northern Mariana Islands established.

OPPOSING PLANS

THE AMERICAN PLAN – OPERATION FORAGER

On 15 January 1944, Marine V Amphibious Corps (VAC) was assigned responsibility for the Marianas operation, "Forager". With the neutralization of Truk and the sudden increased tempo in the Central Pacific, Adm Nimitz directed on 13 March that the operation's planning be given the highest priority.

The Japanese defended the five largest islands of the Marianas in strength. It was decided that Saipan, the second largest and the main stronghold, would be the first target with D-Day set for 15 June. J-Day for Tinian was not specified and W-Day[1] for Guam was tentatively set for 18 June. The assault date would be set when the tactical conditions were ideal. Rota and Pagan were to be by-passed.

VAC was assigned the 2nd and 4th Marine Divisions (MarDiv), 27th Infantry Division (InfDiv), and XXIV Corps Artillery and tasked with the Saipan assault. VAC's own corps artillery had been assigned to take part in the assault on Rabaul, New Britain, but this operation was canceled and it was subsequently attached to XXIV Corps to participate in the Leyte assault. To seize Guam, III Amphibious Corps (IIIAC) was assigned the 3rd MarDiv, 1st Provisional Marine Brigade (Prov MarBde), and 77th InfDiv (the latter initially serving as the General Reserve for the Marianas). VAC was designated the Northern Troops and Landing Force

Much of the southern portion of Saipan was flat and covered by low brush. Here 165th Infantry troops approach Aslito Airfield on 18 June. Much of Saipan was served by a narrow-gauge railroad.

A Japanese narrow-gauge steam locomotive outside of Charan Kanoa. Intended to haul sugarcane, Seabees refurbished locomotives, rolling stock, and track establishing a supply line between the town and Aslito Airfield.

(NTLF) while IIIAC was the Southern Troops and Landing Force (STLF). To control both corps/forces, Lieutenant General Holland M. Smith, Commanding General, VAC, was designated Commanding General, Expeditionary Troops. On 12 April he split the already under-strength VAC staff into the Blue Staff for the Expeditionary Troops and the Red Staff for the NTLF. In some instances principal staff officers served on both staffs augmented by Army officers.

Since there were only 35 days between the formation of the Expeditionary Troops and NTLF and the final rehearsals on 17 May, all echelons immediately began simultaneous planning. Time did not allow the luxury of each echelon making its plans and passing them down. NTLF would initially be the lead force. Its success on Saipan would dictate all subsequent operations along with the employment of the reserve and STLF, with the latter also serving as a reserve for the NTLF until 25 June. The 77th InfDiv initially remained in Hawaii as the Area Reserve, but would later be committed to Guam.

Two sets of beaches, "Scarlet" and "Black", were available on Saipan's upper northwest coast. The "Scarlet" beaches were inside well-defended Tanapag Harbor. The "Black" beaches were farther north near Makunsha Village, but were ill suited for large unit landings. They were designated as alternate beaches and could be used for future supporting landings. The "Brown" beaches on the northeast coast of the Kagman Peninsula near Chacha Village were rejected as being too well defended and offering poor exits. The primary beaches were on Saipan Lagoon, on the southern west coast. The landing beaches were separated by Afetna Point, "Red" and "Green" to the north, and "Blue" and "Yellow" to the south. "Green 3" was actually south of the point, but was not used. These beaches allowed the four assault regiments of two divisions to land simultaneously. The fringing reefs did not present a significant obstacle because of the availability of amphibian tractors. They would, however, hinder off-loading from landing craft, necessitating the capture and opening of Tanapag Harbor to the north.

Landing on the southern portion of the island allowed immediate capture of Charan Kanoa Airstrip and a comparatively quick seizure of the main Aslito Airfield. These airfields would allow early employment of spotter planes and close air support. First the island's south end would be cleared, providing a secure rear area, and then the divisions would roll north. As the advance pushed north into the island's narrower northern half, exhausted units could be pulled out of the line. Neither Beach "White 1" (located on the southwest coast near Cape Obiam and some 2,000yds (1,829m) from Aslito Airfield) nor Beach "Purple" (located on the north side of Magicienne Bay) would be used.

On 12 June (D-3) over 200 carrier aircraft would attack airfields in the southern Marianas. That same day, bomber raids would begin to

TAPOTCHAU

HILL 500

HILL 600

Rugged hills and ridges dominate Saipan's central spine. Such terrain would make the 27th InfDiv's advances extremely difficult. Viewed from the southeast over the west end of Magicienne Bay is 1,554ft (474m) Mt. Tapotchau, the island's highest elevation. Hills 500 and 600 (feet above sea level) were hotly contested by the Japanese. The latter formed the south end of Purple Heart Ridge.

batter Saipan and Tinian, continuing right up to the landings. Carrier fighter-bombing and strafing strikes would continue every day. On the 13th (D-2) battleships and cruisers would begin shelling both islands. At night destroyers would move close inshore and continue the shelling. Besides attacking coastal defense guns, antiaircraft (AA) guns, beach and coastal defenses, airfields, and other installations, white phosphorus rounds would be fired into the cane fields to burn them off.

Underwater Demolition Teams (UDT) would begin reconnoitering the landing beaches, blasting gaps in the reef, marking boat and tank lanes, and demolishing obstacles and mines on the morning of D-1. The NTLF plan called for the two divisional reserve regiments to conduct a demonstration off the "Scarlet" and "Black" beaches with the aim of forcing the enemy to commit reserves and fire support to the north, away from the main landing. Prior to H-Hour naval gunfire could only engage targets within 1,000yds of the shore. Only aircraft would attack inland targets.

The 2nd MarDiv would land north of Afetna Point with the 6th Marines on Beaches "Red 1–3" and the 8th Marines on Beaches "Green 1–2", seize the Charan Kanoa Airstrip, and swing northeast and attack toward Mt. Tipo Pale and the dominating Mt. Tapotchau. This would establish the Landing Force Beachhead Line (LFBL). The 4th MarDiv would land south of Afetna Point with the 23rd Marines on Beaches "Blue 1" and "Blue 2" and the 25th Marines on "Yellow 1–3", seize Charan Kanoa, sever the island by thrusting across to Magicienne Bay, secure Aslito Airfield, and clear the island's south end in a very short time. It would then move north and take up position on the LFBL to 2nd MarDiv's right to take part in the push north. Each battalion would land on an individual numbered beach 600yds wide. Each division was assigned three amphibian tractor battalions and a fourth with amphibian tanks to lead it ashore. It would be the largest use of amtracs to date and would set the standard for future operations. By nightfall on D-Day they were to seize the O-1 Line (Objective) 1,200– 1,500yds (1097–1372m) inland to secure the low ridge dominating the beaches.

NTLF proposed an unprecedented tactic of the troop-carrying Landing Vehicles, Tracked (LVT – amtracs) and amphibian tanks continuing to advance inland beyond the Tractor Control Line, a railroad track 200–700yds (183–640m) inland, and delivering their troops to the O-1 Line. The 4th MarDiv optimistically accepted the proposal. The unit's experiences on low and level Roi-Namur, during the Kwajalein assault, no doubt made this an acceptable idea. The 2nd MarDiv on the other hand, having fought on rugged Guadalcanal and experienced the limitations of LVTs during the Tarawa assault, was more pessimistic. MajGen Watson convinced LtGen Smith that he would only allow the amphibian tanks to advance inland far enough to clear the immediate beach area and that only the first troop-carrying LVT wave would follow them to discharge their troops beyond the beach. All subsequent waves would discharge troops on the beach and not proceed beyond the Tractor Control Line.

The reason for this pessimism was that the Marines expected the terrain to be rougher than some predicted. They feared control would be lost over troops embarked in LVTs, concentrated groups of men would be exposed to fire, and that more amtracs would be lost to enemy fire inland. They were needed to return to the Transfer Control Line on the reef's lip where support troops boated aboard LCVPs would be picked up and run to shore in the amtracs.

LVTs are not designed for cross-country movement. They have comparatively narrow tracks and low ground clearance, making it easy for them to "belly-out" on rough ground, rocks, and stumps. Amphibian tanks are poor substitutes for medium tanks for the same reasons, and in addition they have very thin armor and a high profile.

An unusual operation was planned for the night of D-1 under NTLF control. The Eastern Landing Group consisting of 1/2 Marines and Company A, Amphibious Reconnaissance Battalion, VAC would land on Beach "Purple" and then move rapidly cross-country to seize the peak of Mt. Tapotachau, using it to direct naval gunfire and defending the position until relieved. This was an extremely risky mission and nothing like it had previously been attempted. The 2nd MarDiv staff opposed

Sugarcane fields, especially on Tinian, of which 90 percent was covered by the dense tangled growth, proved to be extremely tough going for tired infantrymen. Regardless of extensive searches, numerous Japanese were able to hide in the fields long after the battle.

this mission and urged NTLF to cancel it. It was feared that the Group might be annihilated in the five days it was predicted it would take 2nd MarDiv to reach Mt. Tapotachau. In the event it was 10 days before the feature was secured. The mission was wisely cancelled on 20 May, but since the Group was embarked on destroyer-transports and its supplies and heavy weapons aboard carriers, it remained under NTLF-control as a reserve for special landing opportunities.

The 27th InfDiv had the most daunting planning effort. As the Expeditionary Force Reserve it had to be prepared to land on 2nd or 4th MarDivs' beaches, the northwest shore's alternate beaches, Magicienne Bay, and on Tinian or Guam. The Division prepared 22 different plans. This meant that every regiment, battalion, and other divisional units developed a like number of plans.

The 2nd and 4th MarDivs would push north to clear the remainder of the island. It was fully realized that the 27th InfDiv would probably be committed to complete the clearing of the south end, placed in the frontline, or conduct a landing on the north side of Magicienne Bay to secure the east flank of the LFBL. In that case the 1st Prov MarBde[2] with STLF would become the NTLF Reserve until released for Guam. On 15 June while en route to Saipan the 106th Infantry was detached from the Division and attached to the 1st Prov MarBde for Guam, but it was released back to the Division just after the Saipan landing.

The plan was for the south end of Saipan to be secured rapidly. Most Japanese resistance would be crushed there and the rest of the island would be secured with relative ease.

Only tentative plans were prepared for Tinian, mainly in the form of continued bombardment and selecting landing beaches. Detailed landing plans would be developed at a later date. The island's inevitable assault was not ignored while the battle for Saipan was under way. NTLF held daily conferences on Tinian. Very accurate mapping was accomplished prior to the assault and additional intelligence had been gleaned from documents captured on Saipan.

THE JAPANESE PLAN –
A-GO OPERATION

The IGHQ established the National Defense Zone, or "Tojo Line", in September 1943 after the loss of eastern New Guinea and the Solomons. In March, after Kwajalein had fallen, the IJN expected the Marianas to be attacked by the end of the month. By April, with the capture or bypassing of the Marshalls, the neutralization of Truk, and the capture of the Admiralties, the IJN assessed that the next strike would be in the Palaus or elsewhere in the Western Carolines. The continued advance westward of MacArthur's forces along the north New Guinea coast reinforced this assessment. The IJA issued orders to reinforce the Marianas in March, but most units would not arrive until May allowing little time to prepare defenses. By June even the IJA felt the next American attack would probably be in the Palaus and even issued orders transferring some personnel from the Marianas. Although these were never put into effect, if they had there would have been 2,500 fewer troops on Saipan.

On 3 May the IGHQ issued plans for the *A-Go* Operation. The Combined Fleet was prepared to execute the long awaited decisive engagement of the invading US Fleet in the Palaus–Carolines area. Land-based aircraft, IJN and IJA, in the Philippines, Carolines, Palaus, and Marianas would be prepared to support this operation. Some 540 land-based aircraft were deployed to the Mandate in June, including 35 to Saipan, 67 to Tinian, and 70 to Guam. After withdrawing from Truk, the Combined Fleet was based at Tawitawi off Borneo's north coast at the southwest end of the Philippines' Sulu Archipelago. This deployment would allow it to sail south of Mindanao or directly to the Western Carolines where possible US targets might be Yap or Woleai. The Combined Fleet could also take one of the numerous passages through the Philippines if American operations proceeded further westward into the northern Netherlands East Indies. The southern Marianas though were a good deal farther from Tawitawi and fuel was short.

On 1 June IGHQ was expecting some move by the US in the Central Pacific. MacArthur's forces had landed on Biak on 27 May, however, placing him only 800 miles (1,287km) from the southern Philippines. The Japanese thought that this might now be the main Allied thrust. This idea had been reinforced by the all-out use of carriers during the Hollandia, New Guinea, landing in April.

The 4th Fleet had been solely responsible for the defense of the Mandates. On 10 March the IJN established the Central Pacific Area Fleet to oversee the Volcano and Bonin Islands north of the Marianas, the Marianas themselves, and the Western Carolines. The 4th Fleet was subordinate to this administrative command. It still had direct control over Truk, the Eastern Carolines, and in theory the bypassed islands in the Marshalls. In theory the Central Pacific Area Fleet also had control of IJA units in the area. The 31st Army, headquartered on Saipan, had been raised at the same time as the new fleet and placed in command of all IJA units in the Central Pacific Area Fleet's zone of command. The 31st Army refused to be subordinate to the IJN, but on 15 March an

For the first time the Marines and Army experienced large numbers of enemy civilians who had to be interned, screened, and cared for. Many were employed as laborers and paid and they and their families were provided food, shelter, and medical care. On Saipan an internment camp was set up near Lake Susupe and on Tinian behind Tinian Town.

This 150mm coast defense gun was one of a battery of three southeast of Tinian Town that fired on the battleship USS *Colorado* and the destroyer USS *Norman Scott* inflicting enough damage that both were withdrawn from the gun line for repairs. The guns had been so well concealed that they had not been detected until they opened fire on J-1. These were British-made 6in. guns purchased by Japan in 1905.

agreement was reached by which the command of each island was under the authority of the senior IJA or IJN commander and that neither the 31st Army or Central Pacific Area Fleet commander would assume overall authority over the area. Thus, there was no unified Japanese command in the Central Pacific and no coordination or joint planning between the IJA and IJN elements on any given island.

The Japanese had previously defended other Central Pacific islands on the beach with the intent of destroying the enemy at the water's edge. The atoll islands were extremely small, providing no space for reserves to maneuver or even second lines of defense, especially since an airfield occupied much of the island. Artillery positions had to be placed on the shoreline and could not be deployed in depth. This did allow them to be used as anti-boat guns, but the ability to conduct concentrated barrages was lost. The level islands lacked dominating terrain features on which to establish in-depth defenses.

The larger hilly islands in the Marianas provided the opportunity to establish defenses in greater depth in multiple lines, develop strongpoints on key terrain, and allow centrally positioned reserves to maneuver to counterattack. The Japanese were unable to take advantage of most of these factors, however. Sufficient forces did not arrive on the islands until less than two months before the US assault. This did not allow adequate time to prepare inland defenses in multiple lines. Numerous coast defense and AA guns were found still in their packing beside unfinished positions. Insufficient construction materials were available to build hardened positions. As it was, the high ground on the island's center had not been prepared for defense and many of the beach defenses were not complete. Too great a reliance was placed on the degree to which the island's rough terrain would slow the Americans. However, many of the coast defense guns were placed in reinforced concrete positions built earlier. Saipan and Tinian had few manmade underwater or beach obstacles, but some use was made of mines on the beaches.

Often, arriving units had lost large numbers of troops to submarine attacks. These units were incomplete, lacked essential equipment and weapons, and time did not allow them to reorganize as cohesive units. The Japanese did establish mobile reserves, but because of the size of the islands and the necessity to defend multiple beaches, they were too small. American air superiority usually prevented them from immediately counterattacking the morning landing. They waited until night, by which time the Americans were well established and prepared to meet the

JAPANESE DEFENSES, SAIPAN

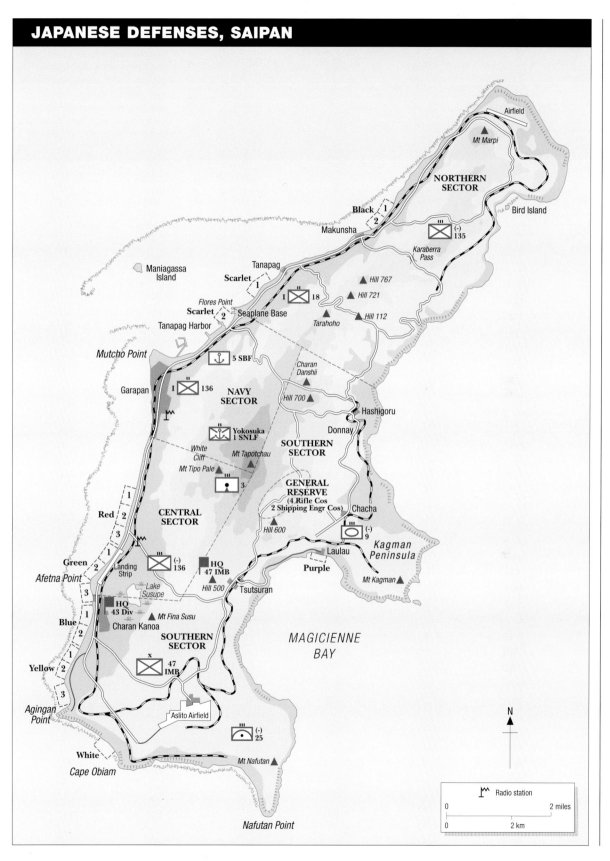

Airfield

Mt Marpi

NORTHERN SECTOR

Bird Island

Black | 1 / 2

Makunsha

Karaberra Pass

⊠ (-) 135

Maniagassa Island

Tanapag

Scarlet | 1

Hill 767

Hill 721

Flores Point

I ⊠ 18

Scarlet | 2 | Seaplane Base

Tarahoho

Hill 112

Tanapag Harbor

Mutcho Point

⚓ 5 SBF

Charan Danshii

Garapan

I ⊠ 136

NAVY SECTOR

Hill 700

Hashigoru

Donnay

⚓ Yokosuka 1 SNLF

SOUTHERN SECTOR

White Cliff

Mt Tapotchau

Mt Tipo Pale

▦ 3

GENERAL RESERVE
(4 Rifle Cos
2 Shipping Engr Cos)

Chacha

1

Red | 2

3

CENTRAL SECTOR

Hill 600

⊡ (-) 9

Kagman Peninsula

Laulau

1

Green | 2

Landing Strip

⊠ (-) 136

■ HQ 47 IMB

Purple

Mt Kagman

Afetna Point

3

Lake Susupe

Hill 500

Tsutsuran

1

Blue | 2

■ HQ 43 Div

▲ Mt Fina Susu

Charan Kanoa

MAGICIENNE BAY

SOUTHERN SECTOR

1

Yellow | 2

⊠ x 47 IMB

3

Agingan Point

Aslito Airfield

⊡ (-) 25

White

Cape Obiam

Mt Nafutan

N ▲

ᨓ Radio station

0 _____ 2 miles

0 _____ 2 km

Nafutan Point

21

inadequate and often uncoordinated attacks. A problem plaguing the 31st Army was the insufficient supplies of AA ammunition on all islands under its control.

As bleak as the Japanese tactical defense situation was, at the operational level it was even more dismal. The *A-Go* Operation, besides relying on the success of the Combined Fleet to defeat the US invasion fleet, counted on land-based aircraft to launch repeated attacks and provide air cover. In the Marianas orders were issued for a total of 14 airfields and two seaplane bases to be built and completed by April. Only nine airfields and the two seaplane bases were completed. Most of the fields hosted 48 aircraft for a theoretical total of 600, but the operational fields could support only 400. Regardless, American air attacks and naval bombardment destroyed all aircraft on the ground or in the air prior to D-Day. Another feature of Japanese operational defense was to establish amphibious reserves on area islands. When the Americans attacked an island the reserves were to be transported by landing barges to either conduct counter-landings or reinforce the defenders. This was somewhat effective in the Solomons with numerous islands in close proximity with barges infiltrating at night. Among the widely spread atolls of the Central Pacific this proved impossible because of the distances and lack of places to hide en route. Air and sea patrols easily interdicted most reinforcement efforts.

Defense of Saipan

For the defense of Saipan the Japanese had 13 infantry battalions assigned to an infantry division and an independent mixed brigade, a battalion-size tank regiment, three artillery battalions, two 320mm mortar battalions, plus various engineer and service units reorganized to some extent as rifle units. There were also 11 IJN coast defense companies, a few IJA and IJN AA units, plus a battalion-size Special Naval Landing Force (SNLF) unit.

The Northern Marianas Army Group, under the command of the 43rd Division, divided Saipan into four defense sectors. The Northern Sector, about one-third of the island, was the responsibility of the 135th Infantry Regiment (-). Also in this sector was I/18 Infantry tasked

This 120mm Type 10 (1921) dual-purpose gun was captured by the 27th InfDiv at Aslito Airfield. Originally designed for shipboard use, it was widely used as an antiaircraft gun ashore and mounted on a concrete mounting in an open emplacement. Some Japanese antiaircraft guns were employed in the direct fire role against ground targets.

with conducting a counter-landing on any American beachhead. Provided with 35 boats it was also to reinforce Tinian if necessary. The Naval Sector encompassed Tanapag Bay and Garapan and was held by 5th Special Base Force units and the SNLF, augmented by I/136 Infantry. The Central Sector, to the south of the Naval Sector, was defended by the 136th Infantry Regiment (-). The Southern Sector covered the lower eastern section of the island and the entire south end and was held by the 47th IMB and the General Reserve. The latter, with four rifle (two from III/136 Infantry and two from III/9 IMR) and two companies from 16th Shipping Engineer Regiment, was positioned in a valley between Mt. Tapotchau and Magicienne Bay. The Japanese CP was initially in a Charan Kanoa schoolhouse, but when the Marines landed it was moved to an unnamed hill northwest of Hill 500. On the 19th it relocated to a cave on a ridge behind Chacha Village and on the 24th to the east side of Mt. Tapotchau. Some artillery was concentrated around Mt. Tapotchau with more to the south behind Hill 500 near Tsutsuran Village. The three battalions were insufficient and the two mortar battalions possessed few weapons. The battalion-sized 25th AAA Regiment (-) was positioned around Aslito Airfield with its attached 43rd Independent AA Company and 44th Field Machine Cannon Company covering central Saipan. Five IJN coast defense companies were sited along the west coast and a sixth on Managassa Island in Tanapag Harbor. Four companies covered Magicienne Bay and another was on Nafutan Point on the southeast end.

The Japanese were prepared for landings on the lower west coast, upper northwest coast, Tanapag Harbor, and north shore of Magicienne Bay. Units were dug into light beach defenses and on high ground overlooking beaches. Strongpoints covered possible landing beaches and were from a few hundred meters to 1km apart. A second line of strongpoints was established inland, the distance inland depending on the terrain. Machine-guns and mortars covered gaps between strongpoints. Dummy strongpoints were constructed. Most of the 9th Tank Regiment's 48 tanks were to assemble 2 miles (3.2km) east of Garapan if the landing

These reinforced concrete air raid shelters were located around Airfield No. 1 on Tinian. They had been destroyed by naval gunfire and dive-bombing. Note the heavily reinforced blast walls protecting the entrances.

occurred at Garapan or Tanapag Harbor. If the landing were conducted at Charan Kanoa or Magicienne Bay, the tanks would assemble ¹/₂-mile (800m) north of Aslito Airfield. One company though was positioned within Charan Kanoa. A major problem faced by the Japanese artillery was the lack of trucks or horses. As such it could only be moved by hand and, this being largely impractical, the Japanese would lose most of their artillery early in the battle. Initially it was very effectively employed and slowed the effort to secure southern Saipan.

Defense of Tinian

Despite the fact that a mere 3 miles (4.8km) separated Tinian and Saipan, there was little planning for mutual support. A 150mm coast defense gun company on the south end of Saipan and 120mm and 140mm companies on the north end of Tinian covered the Saipan Straits, but other long-range artillery was not coordinated. Plans for amphibious reinforcement or counter-landings were made. The Saipan-based I/135 Infantry was caught on Tinian during such an exercise when the Americans arrived. However, only minimal reinforcement attempts from Tinian were made during the battle.

While Tinian is comparatively small, its defense presented the Japanese with several problems. It was mostly flat with few significant terrain features on which to establish defenses. To the north, Mt. Lasso provided observation of much of the island and it was here the Japanese CP was located. There was also some cave-riddled high ground on the south end. Neither of these features though was in a position immediately adjacent to any of the possible beaches. The extensive road system allowed easy access to all areas of the island, but being mostly flat and devoid of concealing vegetation, movement was exposed to attack.

Much of the coastline was edged with low cliffs and this made it easier for the Japanese to position their defenses. The most likely beaches, "Orange", "Red", "Green" and "Blue", were on the southwest coast in the gentle curve of Sunharon Bay. The second most likely landing beach was "Yellow" in Asiga Bay on the northern east coast. This meant that the two most likely landing areas were on opposite sides of the island and reserves would have to be split. There were two tiny beaches, "White 1"

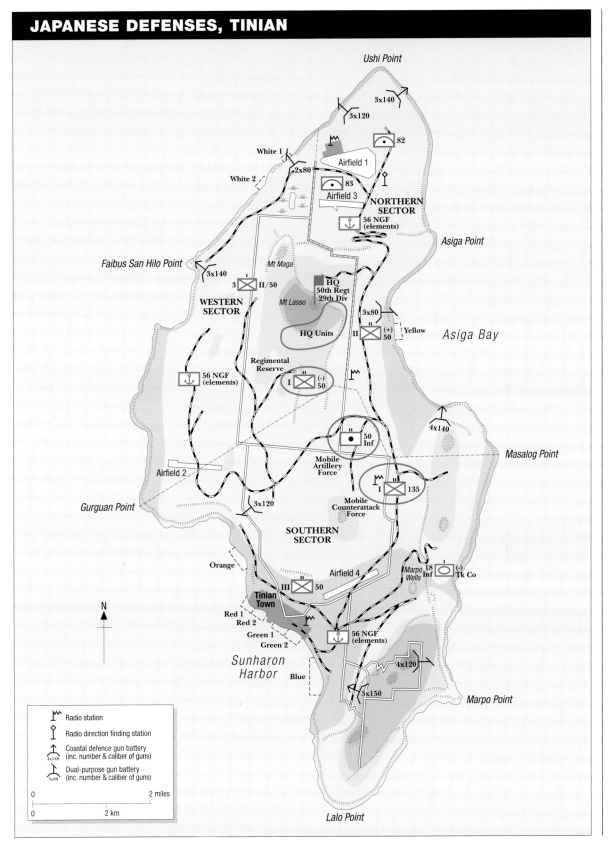

Ushi Point

3x140

3x120

· 82

White 1

2x80

Airfield 1

White 2

· 83

Airfield 3

NORTHERN
SECTOR

Asiga Point

56 NGF
(elements)

Faibus San Hilo Point

3x140

Mt Maga

HQ
50th Regt
29th Div

3x80

WESTERN
SECTOR

3   II/50

Mt Lasso

HQ Units

II   (+)
50   Yellow

Asiga Bay

56 NGF
(elements)

Regimental
Reserve

I   (-)
50

4x140

Masalog Point

· 50
Inf

Mobile
Artillery
Force

I   135

Airfield 2

Mobile
Counterattack
Force

Gurguan Point

3x120

SOUTHERN
SECTOR

Orange

Airfield 4

Marpo
Wells   18
Inf   (+)
Tk Co

III   50

Tinian
Town

Red 1
Red 2

Green 1
Green 2

56 NGF
(elements)

4x120

Sunharon
Harbor   Blue

3x150

Marpo Point

N

Lalo Point

Radio station

Radio direction finding station

Coastal defence gun battery
(inc. number & caliber of guns)
4x140

Dual-purpose gun battery
(inc. number & caliber of guns)
3x80

0   2 miles

0   2 km

and "White 2", on the northwest coast, but the Japanese commander discounted these.

The commander of the 50th Infantry divided Tinian into three defense sectors. The Southern Sector covered about half of the island. 3/50 defended the 2,100yds (1,911m) of beaches fronting Tinian Town on Sunharon Bay. To the northeast of the town I/135 served as the Mobile Counterattack Force while the 12 tanks of Tank Company, 18th Infantry Regiment were positioned east of Airfield No. 4. The Mobile Counterattack Force would be prepared to "advance rapidly to the place of landings, depending on the situation, and attack." The Northern Sector comprised a narrow strip along the upper east coast and protected Airfields No. 1 and 3 as well as Asiga Bay, defended by II/50 (+). The Western Sector covered most of the northwest coast and was defended only by 3rd Company, II/50 (+). I/50 (-) was positioned south of Mt. Lasso as the Regimental Reserve and was to serve as a counterattack force for Asiga Bay or backup for the Mobile Counterattack Force. The battalions defending the beaches were to be prepared to shift two-thirds of their unit to other sectors if the main landings occurred elsewhere. The 50th Infantry's Artillery Battalion and the infantry battalions' 70mm gun platoons constituted the Mobile Artillery Force located near the Mobile Counterattack Force. It was to support that force and the tank company executing counterattacks. The IJN 82nd and 83rd AA Defense Units were positioned around Airfields No. 1 and 3 on the north end. Nine 56th Guard Force coast defense gun companies were positioned around the island protecting Sunharon and Asiga Bays and the northwest coast. Besides beach defenses, strongpoints were established inland. The 50th Infantry had arrived on Tinian in March giving it more time to prepare defenses. They also had the advantage of continuing work on defenses until the landing on Tinian, almost six weeks after the Saipan assault began.

While relations between IJA and IJN forces in the Marianas were strained, on Tinian they were nonexistent. Examination of 50th Infantry and 56th Guard Force plans and orders demonstrate that all plans were made completely independent of the other.

A 27th InfDiv M4A2 Sherman medium tank is lowered into a landing craft, mechanized Mk III (LCM(3)). The tank is fitted with MT-S fording stacks. The LCM would be run to the edge of the coral reef and then the tank would wade ashore following a route marked by UDT frogmen. This provides a good view of the LCM's pilothouse and its two .50-cal M2 machine-guns.

---

1 Each island was assigned a different letter identifying its assault date to prevent confusion between operations.
2 The Brigade was composed of the 4th and 22nd Marines and 4th Amphibian Tractor Battalion.

OPPOSING COMMANDERS

Vice Adm Richmond K. Turner, one of the pioneers of Navy amphibious warfare, was commander of both the Joint Expeditionary Force (TF 51) and the Northern Attack Force (TF 52) as well as commander of Amphibious Force, Fifth Fleet. He oversaw all amphibious operations for Saipan, Tinian, and Guam.

AMERICAN COMMANDERS

Vice Admiral Richmond K. Turner (US Navy) had graduated from the Naval Academy in 1908. He served on battleships during the Great War, but in 1926 he made a major career change and was rated a Naval Aviator. Numerous aviation staff assignments followed, including as executive officer of the carrier USS *Saratoga*, and culminating as Commander, Aircraft, Battle Force of the US Fleet. He next commanded a cruiser and then attended the Naval War College. The opening shots of the war found him as director of the Navy Department's War Plans Division. In the summer of 1942, Turner took over command of amphibious forces in the South Pacific. His experience on planning staffs and the command of air units and ships of the line were to serve him well as he launched the grueling Solomon Islands campaign. Here, he experienced his only defeat at the Battle of Savo Island. In August 1943, he took command of Fifth Fleet Amphibious Force to perfect landing force operations in the Gilberts and Marshalls. For Saipan and Tinian he was both commander of the Joint Expeditionary Force and Northern Attack Force. He later oversaw the Guam and Okinawa landings and directed all amphibious forces of the Third and Fifth Fleets. After the war, he served as the US Navy representative to the UN Military Staff Committee until retiring in 1947. Turner died in 1961.

Lieutenant General Holland M. Smith (USMC) was a practicing Alabama lawyer until commissioned in the Marine Corps in 1905. He served in the Philippines, Panama, Dominican Republic, and France in World War I. It was in the Dominican Republic that he received his most appropriate nickname, "Howlin' Mad". Smith had read much on the career of Napoleon and attributed his own aggressiveness to assuming Bonaparte's style. He graduated from the War College in 1921 and served in a number of positions other than troop command. These positions, Joint Army–Navy Planning Committee, Marine Corps Schools, Post Quartermaster, Force Marine Officer for the Battle Force, Chief of Staff of the Department of the Pacific, and Director of Operations and Training at Headquarters, Marine Corps, all served to provide him with the experience needed to mold the Fleet Marine Force (FMF) into a premiere amphibious assault force. In 1939 he took command of the 1st MarBde and in 1941 it was expanded into the 1st MarDiv. He soon took command of Amphibious Force, Atlantic Fleet and then Amphibious Corps, Pacific Fleet. This corps was redesignated V Amphibious Corps (VAC) in August 1942. Smith was promoted to lieutenant general in May 1944. Commanding VAC, he was responsible for seizing Tarawa, Makin, Roi-Namur, Kwajalein, and Eniwetok. He was designated Commanding General, Expeditionary Troops for the Marianas. He would relinquish command of VAC in July

1944 and, still in command of Expeditionary Troops, took command of the newly activated Fleet Marine Force (FMF), Pacific, to oversee all theater Marine forces. Smith was extremely controversial, not only because he relieved the commanding officer of the 27th InfDiv of his command, but also through his ruthlessly outspoken criticism of the Army and Navy. Unfortunately this grew to the point where he became a liability to joint operations and LtGen Roy S. Geiger took over command of FMFPac in July 1945. Smith would retire in 1946 and died in 1967.

Major General Harry Schmidt (USMC) was commissioned in the Marine Corps in 1909 from Nebraska, with one of his early assignments being Guam. Schmidt's other overseas postings included the Philippines, Nicaragua, and four tours in China. He graduated from the Army Command and General Staff School in 1932, and served in numerous command, staff and instructor positions including Headquarters, Marine Corps. He was Assistant to the Commandant of the Marine Corps until assuming command of the newly activated 4th MarDiv in August 1942. Under his command the Division seized Roi and Namur Islands before participating in the Saipan assault. He assumed command of VAC on 12 July 1944 to allow LtGen Smith to oversee the Guam operation. He commanded VAC through the rest of the war overseeing the Iwo Jima assault and then landed in Japan for occupation duty. From 1946 he commanded Marine Training and Replacement Command until his retirement in 1948 as a full general. He died in 1968.

MajGen Thomas E. Watson (USMC), from Louisiana, was commissioned in the Marines in 1916. He served in the Dominican Republic on three occasions, China, and Nicaragua. After graduating from the Army War College he served in the War Plans Division, Headquarters, Marine Corps from 1938–42. He then commanded the 3rd MarBde in Western Samoa and then the brigade-sized Tactical Group 1 when it seized Eniwetok. Watson took command of the 2nd MarDiv in April 1944 and led it through the Saipan and Tinian operations and supported the Okinawa operation, although only one-third of the Division served ashore there. In July 1945 he took over as Director of Personnel, Headquarters, Marine Corps. From 1948–50 he commanded FMFPac, after which he retired as a lieutenant general. He died in 1966.

MajGen Clifton B. Cates (USMC) graduated from law school in Tennessee, but immediately joined the Marines in 1916. He fought in France in all the Corps' major actions and was wounded twice. He served in China on two occasions, and as aide-de-camp to President Wilson. He graduated from the Army Industrial College in 1932 and the Army War College in 1939. Cates commanded the 1st Marines on Guadalcanal and then served as Commandant of Marine Corps Schools until 1944. He was rushed to Saipan and assumed command of the 4th MarDiv on 12 July when Schmidt took over VAC. In less than two weeks the Division participated in the Tinian assault. He went on to command the Division during the Iwo Jima assault and brought it back to the States for deactivation. He was then President of the Marine Corps Equipment Board and then Commanding General of Marine Barracks, Quantico. In 1948 he was promoted to general and was Commandant of the Marine Corps until 1952. A catch in the law prevented his retirement and he reverted to lieutenant general to again serve as Commandant of Marine Corps Schools. He retired as a full general in 1954 and died in 1970.

LtGen Holland M. Smith ("Howlin' Mad") commanded both Expeditionary Troops (TF 56) for the Marianas campaign and VAC. He relinquished command of VAC in July 1944 and, still in command of Expeditionary Troops, took command of the newly activated FMFPac.

MajGen Harry Schmidt initially commanded the 4th MarDiv, but assumed command of VAC on 12 July to allow LtGen Smith to directly oversee the Guam operation.

The commanding generals of the 4th and 2nd MarDivs meet to discuss further plans on Tinian on J+2. MajGen Clifton B. Cates (left) had assumed command of the 4th MarDiv on 12 July when Schmidt took over VAC. MajGen Thomas E. Watson (right) commanded the 2nd MarDiv through both the Saipan and Tinian operations.

MajGen Ralph C. Smith (US Army), from Nebraska, had graduated from Officer Candidate School in 1916, served briefly on the Mexican border, and fought in World War I. After the war he attended the Command and General Staff School, War College, and the French *l'École de Guerre*. His attendance at these schools was interspersed by infantry command and instructor assignments. He was assigned to the Military Intelligence Division from 1938 to 1942 and was then assistant division commander of the 76th InfDiv. He took command of the 27th InfDiv in November 1942 in Hawaii. At the time the 27th was assigned an outer Hawaiian islands defense mission. He took the Division through its combat training program and personally led the 165th Infantry Northern Attack Force that seized Makin Atoll in February 1944. LtGen Holland Smith relieved him of command on 24 June, 10 days into the Saipan assault. Ralph Smith was reassigned as commander of the 98th InfDiv in Hawaii, but due to the rift this affair caused in the Pacific Theater, he was reassigned to the Infantry Replacement Training Center, Camp J.T. Robinson, Arkansas. At the end of 1944 he was reassigned as Military Attaché to the reopened US Embassy in Paris until retiring in 1946. Smith died in 1999 at the age of 102. The post-war National Guard training camp at Peekskill, NY, was named after him.

MajGen Sanderford Jarman (US Army), a Coast Artillery officer from Louisiana, had graduated from West Point in 1904. He served in numerous Coast Artillery assignments including command of such units in Panama and Hawaii as well as serving on the War Department General Staff. From 1941 to 1944 he commanded Antiaircraft Command, Eastern Defense Command. He was designated Commanding General, US Army Garrison Force, Saipan, and would assume command of the island once it was declared secure with responsibility for mopping-up, defense, administration, and base development. As the senior Army officer on Saipan, LtGen Holland Smith had confided in Jarman the day before

RIGHT **MajGen Ralph C. Smith commanded the 27th InfDiv until relieved by LtGen Smith on 24 June, creating a great deal of controversy and a rift between the Army and Marine Corps.**

FAR RIGHT **MajGen Sanderford Jarman commanded US Army Garrison Force, Saipan and assumed command of the 27th InfDiv when MajGen Smith was relieved on 24 June. He resumed command of the Garrison Force on 28 June after the arrival of MajGen Griner. Pictured to the right of Jarman is LtGen Robert C. Richardson, Jr. Commanding General, US Army Forces, Central Pacific Area.**

relieving MajGen Ralph Smith that he may have to do so. Jarman was temporarily placed in command of the 27th InfDiv on 24 June when MajGen Smith was relieved. He had no experience commanding large maneuver formations and only reluctantly accepted. On the 28th he resumed command of the Garrison Force when MajGen Griner took command of the Division. Jarman remained in command of the Garrison Force until April 1945. He retired in 1946 and died in 1954.

MajGen George W. Griner (USA) was from Georgia and was commissioned in the infantry in 1917, serving in World War I. Between the wars he held various infantry (to include in the Philippines), staff, and ROTC instructor assignments. He became Assistant Division Commander, 77th InfDiv and soon took command of the 13th Airborne Division. He was in command of the 98th InfDiv in Hawaii at the time MajGen Ralph Smith was relieved of his command, and he was quickly flown to Saipan and took command of the 27th InfDiv on 28 June. Griner remained in command of the Division, which fought on Okinawa, until it was deactivated in December 1945, but felt the Division's officers never fully accepted him. Griner retired in 1946 and died in 1974.

MajGen George W. Griner took over command of the 27th InfDiv on 28 June.

JAPANESE COMMANDERS

The Japanese command structure in the Marianas was somewhat disjointed at the time of the invasion. The 31st Army commander was in the Palaus on an inspection tour. With no deputy commander and the chief of staff being junior to the 43rd Division commander, the latter assumed command of the Northern Marianas Army Group. Two vice admirals were present, but neither assumed formal command of Imperial Japanese Navy (IJN) Land Forces on the islands, leaving the rear admiral commanding 5th Special Base Force in control of operations.

LtGen Obata Hideyoshi (IJA) commanding the 31st Army was caught in the Palaus on an inspection trip when the Americans arrived at Saipan. Obata had graduated from the Army War College in 1919 after being commissioned in the cavalry in 1911. He was a military student in Britain in the 1920s and held a number of staff, instructor, and cavalry command assignments. In 1935 he went into aviation and commanded various air units. His 5th Air Group attacked the Philippines on 9 December 1941 and was soon fighting in Burma. He later commanded the 3rd Air Army and was then on the Army General Staff. He took command of the 31st Army in March 1944. It was envisioned that the defense of the islands would be conducted largely by air units. Obata was able to make it to Guam and established a new skeleton headquarters. He still had authority over Saipan and Tinian, but was able to have little impact on the battle. The American command was initially unaware of Obata's presence on Guam. With the death of the 29th Division commander on 26 July, Obata took direct command of forces on Guam. He committed suicide on 11 August as US troops overran his command post, and was later posthumously promoted to full general.

LtGen Saito Yoshitsugu (IJA) commanded the 43rd Division and doubled as Commander, Northern Marianas Army Group. Very little is known of this officer's career prior to his posting to Saipan. It is known only that he was a cavalry officer and had previously commanded a

LtGen Obata Hideyoshi, commanding general of the 31st Army responsible for the defense of the Mariana Islands.

remount unit in Japan. He committed suicide on 7 July after ordering the largest *banzai* change of the war.

Col Ogata K.[3] **(IJA)** commanded the 50th Infantry, 29th Division and as such was the senior commander on Tinian. No additional information is available on this officer other than he had served in Manchuria with the 29th Division. He died leading the last counterattack on 31 July.

Rear Adm Tsujimura Takahisa (IJN) commanded the 5th Special Base Force on Saipan and was ostensibly in change of Imperial Japanese Navy (IJN) units on Tinian. Virtually nothing is known of this officer. He died on 16 July, seven days after the island was declared secure.

Vice Adm Nagumo Chiuchi (IJN) graduated from the Naval Academy in 1908 and mainly served aboard destroyers, becoming a torpedo specialist. He graduated from the Naval College in 1929 and then commanded battleships and cruisers. In 1939 he took command of the 1st Air Fleet (carrier aircraft) and was instrumental in developing doctrine for its use. He commanded the Fleet during the Pearl Harbor attack. After participating in other operations, his forces were defeated at Midway in July 1942. Considered a defeatist and too conservative by Adm Yamamoto, he was given command of the 3rd Fleet, a lesser command. He suffered a second defeat during the August battle of Santa Cruz Islands. Nagumo was ordered to return the Fleet to Japan for rebuilding, but was relieved upon arrival. He was given command of Sasebo Naval Base until his posting to the newly raised Central Pacific Area Fleet. He, LtGen Saito, and Rear Adm Yano Hideo (his chief of staff) committed ritual suicide together on 7 July. Nagumo was posthumously promoted to full admiral in December 1944.

Vice Adm Kakuta Kakuji (IJN) (also spelled Katuta) had the misfortune of being caught on Tinian when the Americans arrived. He was on an inspection tour of Central Pacific airbases and was unable to return to his 1st Air Fleet headquarters in Manila. His entire career was as a line officer and he was assigned command of the Air Fleet in October 1942. A reputed alcoholic, he did not exercise command over any forces on Tinian and was thought to lack the fortitude to do so. No details of his death are known other than it may have been around 12 August long after Tinian was secured.

---

3 Virtually every reference provides a different spelling of Ogata's personal name: Kiyoshi, Kiyochi, Keishi, Takashi.

OPPOSING FORCES

US FORCES

The **Joint Expeditionary Force** (Task Force 51) controlled the entire Marianas operation under Vice Adm Richmond K. Turner. This Navy command itself was subordinate to the **Fifth Fleet and Central Pacific Forces** (TF 50) under Vice Adm Raymond A. Spruance. Two other task forces were under TF 50 and supported the Marianas operation**, Fast Carrier Force** (TF 58) under Vice Adm Marc A. Mitschner and **Forward Area, Central Pacific** (TF 57) controlling land-based aircraft under Vice Adm John H. Hover. TF 58 had 15 carriers with 900 aircraft. TF 57 included the Fifth Air Force on Cape Gloucester and New Guinea; Seventh Air Force and 4th Marine Aircraft Wing on Roi, Eniwetok, Tarawa, Makin and Abemama; and Thirteenth Air Force in the Admiralty Islands.

TF 51 included **Northern Attack Force** (TF 52) for Saipan, **Southern Attack Force** (TF 53) for Guam, and **Expeditionary Troops** (TF 56). It also included three task groups as reserves and garrison forces: Joint Expeditionary Reserve (Task Group 51.1) with 27th InfDiv (afloat), Defense and Garrison Groups (TG 52.2 to 51.7), General Reserve (TG 51.8) with 77th InfDiv (Hawaii), and Landing Craft, Tank Flotilla 13 (TG 51.9).

The Expeditionary Troops included two separate task groups, NTLF (TG 56.1) consisting of VAC for Saipan and Tinian and STLF (TG 56.2) with IIIAC for Guam. The 2nd and 4th MarDivs were assigned to VAC along with XXIV Corps Artillery. The 27th InfDiv would be released to NTLF on 16 June.

Three Marine and three Army amphibian tractor battalions would land the 2nd and 4th MarDivs on Tinian on J-Day. They were equipped with 667 landing vehicles, tank Mk II and IV (LVT(2) and (4), the former pictured here) or "amtracs."

Although used earlier, the 2½-ton DUKW-353 amphibian truck ("Duck") was employed in large numbers; some 50 in each in two Army and two Marine amphibian truck companies. Some Ducks were fitted with A-frame hoists for cargo unloading once ashore. Able to carry 5,000lbs of cargo, they were mainly used to haul in light artillery and ammunition.

The three divisions began training for Saipan in the first week of March. Emphasis was given to both day and night exercises with special attention placed on infantry/tank teams as well as calling for and adjusting artillery and naval gunfire. Maneuvers were conducted off Maui from 12 to 31 March for the 2nd MarDiv and 13 to 26 April for the 4th MarDiv. A full rehearsal was conducted at Maui for both Marine divisions from 17 to 20 May and 20 to 23 May for the 27th InfDiv.

All Marine and Army ground forces were up to or over strength, the troops well rested and trained, and morale was high. However, on 21 May the 2nd and 4th MarDivs had lost 95 and 112 men respectively, plus equipment, when six landing ships, tank (LST) caught fire from an ammunition explosion in Pearl Harbor. The men, equipment, and ships were replaced, but the troops had not been trained for the mission. Earlier, three landing craft, tank (LCT), each armed with three 4.2in. mortars, were lost in an accident causing 35 Marine casualties. These were to have provided fire support to 2nd MarDiv's north flank. No replacement mortar craft were available.

Several new weapons were fielded. The truck-mounted 4.5in. Mk 7 multiple rocket launcher, A-H1B "Satan" flamethrower, mounted in the M3A1 light tank, LVT(4) amtrac, and LVT(A)4 amphibian tank. The Army used the 4.2in. M2 mortar, 2.36in. M9 bazooka, and M2-2 flamethrower for the first time in the Pacific. Napalm bombs were dropped on Tinian in their first use in the Pacific.

Ammunition shortages would be experienced on Saipan and Tinian because the combat proved more prolonged and intense than expected. By 1 July some items were rationed. The only severe shortage experienced was mortar ammunition. Captured Japanese 81mm ammunition was often used in US mortars.

US Marine Corps

V Amphibious Corps was activated on 25 August 1943 at Camp Elliott, California, from the old Amphibious Corps, Atlantic Fleet staff as the Fifth Fleet's amphibious force. In September it relocated to Pearl Harbor with MajGen Holland M. Smith in command. With Marine and Army divisions attached, it seized Tarawa and Makin in the Gilberts in November 1943 and Roi and Namur, Kwajalein, and Eniwetok in the Marshalls in February 1944. Tasked as the NTLF for the Marianas operation, it planned, prepared, and trained for the operation in Hawaii. VAC was augmented with Army medical units to total 3,727 corps troops. Among these was VAC Provisional (Prov) LVT Group controlling three Marine and three Army amphibian tractor battalions, a Marine armored amphibian tractor battalion, and an Army amphibian tank battalion for a total of 719 LVTs. VAC Prov Engineer Group coordinated divisional and non-divisional engineer units and naval construction battalions. The 7th Field Depot provided logistical support.

The **2nd Marine Division** was organized from the 2nd Marine Brigade at San Diego, California, on 1 February 1941 (the 2nd MarBde was organized in 1936). As "The Silent Second" trained for deployment, it contributed regiments to serve as defense forces in Iceland and Samoa. The Division's regiments were fed piecemeal into Guadalcanal between August 1942 and January 1943. The Division itself had in the meantime deployed to New Zealand and reassembled there in its entirety after Guadalcanal. The Division, along with the 3rd New Zealand Division, was to have assaulted Rabaul, New Britain, in November 1943, but this operation was cancelled and instead the Division seized Tarawa Atoll, suffering heavy losses. The Division rebuilt on Hawaii and before long began to prepare for the Marianas. Its assault strength was 21,746 troops.

The **4th Marine Division** was activated at Camp Pendleton, California, on 16 August 1943 from existing units and cadres from the 3rd MarDiv. In January 1944 "The Fighting Fourth" departed for Kwajalein Atoll for the longest shore-to-shore amphibious assault in history, 4,300 miles (6,920km), until the British 8,000-mile (12,875km) 1982 Falklands expedition. The Division took Roi and Namur Islands with light losses. It sailed for Maui, Hawaiian Islands and there prepared for the Marianas assault. It would assault with 21,618 troops.

1st Battalion, 29th Marines was organized as the 2nd Separate Infantry Battalion from surplus 2nd MarDiv troops when the Division was reorganized under the new Table of Organization. It was redesignated 1/29 in May while the remainder of the Regiment was organizing in the States. 1/29 would be attached to both the 2nd and 4th MarDivs during the Saipan operation.

Marine regiments are simply given a numerical designation with no branch of service description. Nor is the term "regiment" included in their title. Thus the 2nd Marines might be an infantry regiment, whilst the 10th Marines is an artillery unit and the 18th Marines an engineer regiment.

The infantry regiments committed to this operation were the 2nd, 6th, 8th (2nd MarDiv); 23rd, 24th, 25th (4th MarDiv). The artillery regiments were the 10th and 14th and the engineer regiments the 18th and 20th. For clarity the branch of service will be included in brackets after the designation of Marine artillery and engineer regiments.

The Marine divisions had undergone reorganization in early 1944. The artillery regiment was reduced to four battalions, the special weapons battalion eliminated, and the amphibian tractor battalion reassigned to FMF. The engineer regiment was eliminated, but the 2nd and 4th MarDivs retained theirs as the regiments were integrated into the divisions' plans.

The tank battalion's reconnaissance company was reassigned to the headquarters battalion. At the same time "Light" was dropped from the tank battalions' designation and they received 75mm gun-armed M4A2 Sherman medium tanks to replace their M3A1 light tanks. The tank companies had 15 Shermans. Both of the divisions added a provisional Company D with three platoons, each with six M3A1 flame-tanks and two M5A1 gun-tanks for support.

The 1st and 2nd Battalions had 75mm M1A1 pack howitzers and the 3rd and 4th had 105mm M2A1 howitzers. Artillery batteries had four pieces. The 2nd MarDiv's 10th Marines' 5th Battalion was reorganized and designated 2nd 155mm Howitzer Battalion in April while 4th MarDiv's 14th Marines' 5th Battalion was designated 4th 105mm Howitzer Battalion. The latter though was still called 5/14 Marines during the operation.

The 3,236-man infantry regiments had a 261-man headquarters and service company, 203-man regimental weapons company, and three 954-man infantry battalions. The weapons company had four 75mm M3A1 halftrack-mounted guns and 12 37mm M3A1 AT guns. The infantry battalions lost their weapons companies. The mortar platoon with four 81mm M1 mortars was reassigned to the 213-man headquarters company.

The 240-man rifle companies had a headquarters, three rifle platoons, and a machine-gun platoon. The former company weapons platoon was converted to a machine-gun platoon with six .30cal. M1919A4 air-cooled

Tinian Town, the island's only community, was virtually leveled to reinforce the Japanese belief that the main landing would occur on the beaches fronting the town. Even most of the concrete buildings were flattened.

light and six reserve .30-cal. M1917A1 water-cooled heavy machine-guns (HMG). The latter could be substituted for the light machine-guns (LMG). The mortar section with three 60mm M2 mortars was reassigned to the company headquarters.

Both Marine and Army amphibian tractor battalions had three companies each with 30 LVT(2)s or LVT(4)s or a mix. The Marine 2nd Armored Amphibian Tractor Battalion had four companies with 18 75mm howitzer-armed LVT(A)4 amphibian tanks. The Army's 708th Amphibian Tank Battalion had the same organization, but had older 37mm gun-armed LVT(A)1 amphibian tanks mixed with LVT(A)4s.

A 105th Infantry squad advances toward Ridge 300 on Nafutan Peninsula on Saipan's southeast end, 21 June. Note the bazooka gunner on the right end carrying the two-piece 2.36in. M9 bazooka. To his left his assistant gunner carries extra rockets in an M6 ammunition bag.

US ARMY

The **27th Infantry Division** was initially tasked as the Joint Expeditionary Force Reserve. It would be released to VAC on 15 July to land on Saipan. The "New York Division" was a National Guard unit and had served on the Mexican border in 1916 and fought in World War I. It was inducted into Federal service on 15 October 1940 in New York City and after training in the South it moved to Hawaii where it continued to train and provide outer island defense. The reinforced 165th Infantry assaulted Makin Atoll in November 1943 under VAC. The 106th Infantry had seized Eniwetok with the 22nd Marines as part of VAC's Tactical Group 1 in February and March 1944. 2/106th Infantry secured unoccupied Majuro. After the 106th Infantry's return, training continued and the Division prepared for the Marianas operation. The Division's assigned strength was 16,404 with almost 4,000 attached personnel. Saipan was to be the first combat action for most of the troops.

The 27th InfDiv's attachments included the 1165th Engineer Combat Group with three engineer combat battalions (the 152nd had been organized from the Division's old 2nd Battalion, 102nd Engineer Regiment), some 3,100 troops, to serve as regimental shore parties. Other attachments included a tank battalion and medical units. Besides Army amphibian tractor and medical units supporting the Marines, the Marine divisions had Army Transportation Corps port companies attached to assist the shore parties.

The Army's 2,682-man **XXIV Corps Artillery** replaced VAC Artillery as the latter had been assigned to the cancelled Yap operation. Instead, it accompanied XXIV Corps to Leyte. XXIV Corps Artillery, under BrigGen Arthur M. Harper, controlled two Army 155mm gun and two 155mm howitzer battalions. XXIV Corps Artillery had been organized by redesignating the 225th Field Artillery Group (Motorized) on 31 May in Hawaii. Subordinate to it was the 420th Field Artillery Group, previously the 1st Prov Gun Group, redesignated on 31 May en route to Saipan. For the Tinian assault it would additionally control most of the three divisions' artillery battalions, 14 of the 18 Army and Marine battalions. There was also a 949-man Army Prov Antiaircraft Artillery (AAA) Group with two battalions.

The **77th Infantry Division**[4] was assigned as the Joint Expeditionary Force General Reserve. It initially remained on Hawaii and was not committed to Saipan or Tinian, but could have been if necessary. The "Statue of Liberty Division" was an Army Reserve division largely from New York and New Jersey. Because of severe shipping shortages the Division would not be available for commitment until D+20. The 18,000-man formation was later committed to Guam – its first combat operation.

Army infantry regiments had 3,257 troops in a 108-man headquarters and headquarters company, a 118-man cannon company with two 105mm M7 and four 75mm M8 self-propelled howitzers, a 165-man anti-tank company with nine 37mm M3A1 anti-tank guns, and a 115-man service company. The three 871-man infantry battalions had a 155-man headquarters and service company, three 193-man rifle companies, and a 160-man heavy weapons company with eight .30cal. M1917A1 HMGs and six 81mm M1 mortars. The rifle companies had three 39-man rifle platoons and a weapons platoon with two .30cal. M1919A4 LMGs and three 60mm M2 mortars.

Army division artillery had three 105mm M2A1 howitzer battalions and one with 155mm M1A1 howitzers. The attached 762nd Provisional Tank Battalion had M4A2 Sherman tanks. Companies A and C were

Service troops of the 8th Marines man-pack ammunition up the side of Mt. Tapotchau. Stacked by type in the upper left, it had been brought forward by trucks as trails allowed. While much of Saipan was accessible by road, getting supplies and ammunition to the frontline troops was often an ordeal, as was evacuating casualties.

equipped with 17 tanks each, while Company D had 17 M5A1 light tanks, as did the attached Company D, 766th Tank Battalion.

Both Marine and Army regiments were task organized into regimental combat teams (RCT). The 2nd MarDiv simply referred to them as combat teams (CT). These differed somewhat, even among RCTs within the same division as they were organized for specific missions. They were augmented with tank, combat engineer, and medical companies plus service elements.

JAPANESE FORCES

Northern Marianas Army Group

The **31st Army** had been established in March 1944 to control IJA units in the Mandate. In the IJA an "army" equates to a Western army corps. The 31st Army had little tactical control over its widespread forces. Being responsible for IJA units in the Mandate, it controlled five divisions, six IMBs, and five independent infantry regiments – more than the norm. The Army commander was caught returning from an inspection of the Palaus and was diverted to Guam. He established a new headquarters there while his main headquarters was still on Saipan under the chief of staff.

The **43rd Division** was activated in June 1943 at Nagoya, Japan, from the 63rd Independent Infantry Group. It was deployed to Saipan in late May and early June 1944 in two echelons. The first echelon arrived safely. The second suffered repeated submarine attacks with five of its seven transports sunk. The remaining transports picked up survivors and about 80 percent of the echelon arrived. However, the 118th Infantry had lost 1,400 men and the survivors retained little equipment and were so short of leaders that it was only marginally effective. The division's strength was down to 12,900 and it had no organic artillery.

Other units sent to Saipan suffered from submarine attacks too and as a result there were up to 4,000 unorganized stragglers, many without weapons and little use to the defense. Time was not available to effectively organize and equip them. The 29th Division sailed for Guam at the end of February and one of its three transports was sunk. Of the 3,080 troops of the 18th Infantry, 1,688 were rescued. They landed on Saipan with virtually no weapons or equipment. Some 600 survivors were organized into the I/18 Infantry. The 9th Expeditionary Unit, en route to Yap, lost two transports and the remaining 1,500 troops put ashore on Saipan. Some 600 were organized into the 318th Independent Infantry Battalion (IIB) for the 47th IMB. III/9 Independent Mixed Regiment, bound for Pagan, was also caught on Saipan.

The 1st Expeditionary Unit arrived on Saipan in May with four infantry and two artillery battalions and was reorganized as the **47th Independent Mixed Brigade**. The 47th IMB was to be transferred to Tinian to replace the 50th Infantry, 29th Division, which would then be shipped to Rota. This was to have occurred about 15 July, D-Day. This would have provided a slightly more capable unit to defend Tinian. The Brigade's 315th IIB was on Pagan.

The battalion-size 9th Tank Regiment (less 1st and 2nd and half of 7th Companies) had 36 Type 97 (1937) 57mm medium tanks and 12 Model 95 (1935) 37mm light tanks in its four and a half remaining companies. The 3rd Independent Mountain Artillery Regiment (less II Battalion) had 24 75mm Type 94 (1934) mountain guns and the 25th AAA Regiment (less II Battalion) had eight 75mm Type 88 (1928) AA guns in its remaining I Battalion. There were two independent artillery mortar battalions. Each was supposed to have 16 320mm Type 98 (1938) spigot mortars, but many had been lost and the units were under strength. The 7th Independent Engineer Regiment was a battalion-size fortification construction unit. The 16th Shipping Engineer Regiment operated landing barges. It was reconfigured as a rifle unit.

The 105th Infantry came ashore on the "Yellow" Beaches on J+2. The 165th Infantry had landed the day before on the "Blue" Beaches. The 105th encountered difficulties in landing as most of its organizational equipment was aboard transport that had been ordered to retire eastward because of an airraid warning.

The 29th Division had been shipped to Guam from Manchuria, but its **50th Infantry** was landed on Tinian at the beginning of March. The Division had been raised in August 1941 in Nagoya, Japan. It had been reorganized as a sea operations division, optimized to allow its regiments to operate more effectively on quasi-detached operations on Pacific islands. Allied intelligence referred to this structure as a "regimental combat team" organization. The I/135 Infantry, which had been conducting an amphibious exercise from Saipan and was caught on Tinian, augmented the Regiment when the Americans arrived. Tank Company, 18th Infantry was present with 12 Type 95 (1935) light tanks.

The 43rd Division's regiments consisted of a regimental headquarters with train, signal company, infantry gun company (4 x 75mm Type 41 (1908) regimental guns), AT company (6 x 37mm Type 94 (1934) "AT" guns), and three infantry battalions. A very small number of the more effective 47mm Type 1 (1941) AT gun were available.

A Caterpillar D-18 bulldozer drags two ammunition pallets out of an LCM. The pallet system proved to be effective. They could be loaded and unloaded easily using cranes and dragged by vehicles to dumps, as the bottom braces were sled-like skids. Five-ton crawler cranes were boated ashore to unload cargo from landing craft, DUWKs, and amtracs.

The infantry battalions had a small headquarters with train, machine-gun company (8 or 12 x 7.7mm Type 92 (1932) or Type 1 (1941) HMGs), battalion gun platoon or company (2 or 4 x 70mm Type 92 (1932) battalion guns, respectively), and three or four rifle companies.

The 50th Infantry on Tinian was organized much differently, being a sea operations unit. Each battalion had three rifle companies and an infantry gun platoon with two 70mm battalion guns. Rather than a machine-gun company, each rifle company had a machine-gun platoon with four HMGs. The regiment itself had an organic battalion-size artillery unit of two companies with seven 105mm howitzers and a company with eight 75mm field guns and company-size engineer, signal, supply, and medical units plus an AT platoon with six 37mm guns.

Central Pacific Area Fleet

The Central Pacific Area Fleet had been established in March 1944 for administrative control of IJN elements in the Mandate. The 5th Special Base Force was headquartered on Saipan and oversaw IJN Land Force units on Saipan, Tinian, and Guam. It had been designated 5th Base Force until 10 April 1942 when its responsibilities were expanded. The Central Pacific Area Fleet and 5th Special Base Force headquarters were combined in May. In early 1944 the 2,000-man 55th Guard Force arrived on Saipan to man 11 coast defense gun companies, each armed with from one to three 120mm, 140mm, 150mm, or 200mm guns. The Yokosuka 1st SNLF, a battalion-size parachute unit, arrived in September 1943 with 1,500 troops. Some 700 were transferred to New Britain.

There is some mystery regarding the headquarters of the Sixth Fleet, the Japanese submarine force. It was headquartered on Truk, but is reported to have been relocated to Saipan in the spring of 1944 because of fuel shortages, even though there was no berthing or repair facilities. Vice Admiral Takagi Takeo commanded the Fleet. It is unclear if he was actually on Saipan. He has been reported to have died there and also as having died en route to Saipan aboard a submarine. Ten of its *Ro* submarines were deployed along the *Na* Line northeast of the

27th InfDiv soldiers complete the destruction of one of three pillboxes holding up their advance toward Aslito Airfield on 17 June.

Admiralties to intercept the US fleet as it approached the Carolinas or Marianas.

IJN forces on Tinian included the 1,400-man 56th Guard Force manning nine companies with three or four 80mm, 120mm, 140mm, and 150mm coast defense guns each along with 25mm Type 96 (1936) twin AA guns in an anti-boat role. There were four 400–600-man construction battalions manned by Okinawans and Koreans. The 82nd AA Defense Unit had four 20mm Model 98 (1938) and 24 25mm twin AA guns and the 83rd AA Defense Unit had six 75mm Type 88 (1925) AA guns. A small Coastal Security Force operated patrol boats (all destroyed) and maintained beach mines.

There were a number of naval air service personnel on the island from the 523rd Air Group who were of little tactical value. Many of the air personnel had departed in May and early June to support the reinforcement of Biak. They were ordered to return, but none made it beyond the Palaus.

Japanese forces on Saipan fielded 25,469 IJA and 6,160 IJN, almost double US intelligence estimates. Only 15,000 IJA troops were armed though. On Tinian there were 3,929 IJA and 4,110 IJN personnel.

---

4 Consisted of the 305th, 306th, and 307th Infantry Regiments, 304th, 305th, 306th (155mm), and 902nd Field Artillery Battalions.

CAPTURE AND OCCUPATION OF SAIPAN

Preliminaries

On 25 May 1944 the slow-moving LSTs departed Hawaii for Eniwetok. Because of the fire that destroyed six LSTs they were a day behind schedule. On 29–30 May the troop transports departed Hawaii and the Joint Expeditionary Force assembled at Eniwetok 6–11 June. On the day the first convoy arrived at Eniwetok, TF 58, the Fast Carrier Force, departed Majuro in the Marshalls and headed for the Marianas.

From 11 to 13 June the preparatory naval and air bombardment of Saipan, Tinian, and Guam commenced as did air attacks on Rota and Pagan. On 12 June (D-3) 216 carrier aircraft attacked southern Marianas airfields. The same day B-24 bomber raids began battering Saipan and Tinian. Most sources state 150 Japanese aircraft were destroyed on the ground and in the air, but it appears that only 36 were destroyed. On the 12th and 13th, carrier aircraft interdicted several Japanese convoys fleeing the Marianas sinking 12 cargo ships plus a few escort vessels and large numbers of fishing boats as they might transfer troops between islands. On the 13th, seven 16in. gun-armed fast battleships began shelling both islands. The results were disappointing as the ships were trained for ship-to-ship engagements and not for methodical shore bombardment. Other than leveling Garapan and Charan Kanoa they inflicted little damage. It was a different matter on the 14th when fire support ships with the Northern and Southern Attack Forces joined in the bombardment. The old battleships, 11 cruisers, and 26 destroyers severely pounded the defenses. White phosphorus rounds fired into the cane fields to burn them off were only partly successful because of the

2/105 Infantry troops approach the clifftop of Nafutan Peninsula southeast of Aslito Airfield. On the night of 26 June some 500 Japanese broke out of the peninsula and attacked toward Hill 500 where the 25th Marines were located as the NTLF Reserve. The Japanese force was virtually wiped out. Nafutan Peninsula was declared secure at 18.40hrs, 27 June.

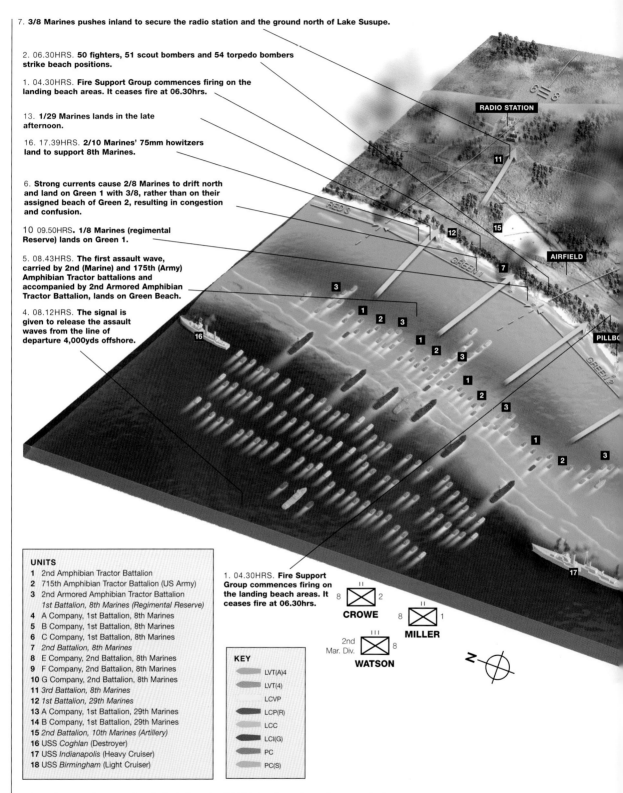

7. **3/8 Marines pushes inland to secure the radio station and the ground north of Lake Susupe.**

2. 06.30HRS. **50 fighters, 51 scout bombers and 54 torpedo bombers strike beach positions.**

1. 04.30HRS. **Fire Support Group commences firing on the landing beach areas. It ceases fire at 06.30hrs.**

13. **1/29 Marines lands in the late afternoon.**

16. 17.39HRS. **2/10 Marines' 75mm howitzers land to support 8th Marines.**

6. **Strong currents cause 2/8 Marines to drift north and land on Green 1 with 3/8, rather than on their assigned beach of Green 2, resulting in congestion and confusion.**

10 09.50HRS. **1/8 Marines (regimental Reserve) lands on Green 1.**

5. 08.43HRS. **The first assault wave, carried by 2nd (Marine) and 175th (Army) Amphibian Tractor battalions and accompanied by 2nd Armored Amphibian Tractor Battalion, lands on Green Beach.**

4. 08.12HRS. **The signal is given to release the assault waves from the line of departure 4,000yds offshore.**

1. 04.30HRS. **Fire Support Group commences firing on the landing beach areas. It ceases fire at 06.30hrs.**

UNITS
1 2nd Amphibian Tractor Battalion
2 715th Amphibian Tractor Battalion (US Army)
3 2nd Armored Amphibian Tractor Battalion
   1st Battalion, 8th Marines (Regimental Reserve)
4 A Company, 1st Battalion, 8th Marines
5 B Company, 1st Battalion, 8th Marines
6 C Company, 1st Battalion, 8th Marines
7 *2nd Battalion, 8th Marines*
8 E Company, 2nd Battalion, 8th Marines
9 F Company, 2nd Battalion, 8th Marines
10 G Company, 2nd Battalion, 8th Marines
11 *3rd Battalion, 8th Marines*
12 *1st Battalion, 29th Marines*
13 A Company, 1st Battalion, 29th Marines
14 B Company, 1st Battalion, 29th Marines
15 *2nd Battalion, 10th Marines (Artillery)*
16 USS *Coghlan* (Destroyer)
17 USS *Indianapolis* (Heavy Cruiser)
18 USS *Birmingham* (Light Cruiser)

KEY
LVT(A)4
LVT(4)
LCVP
LCP(R)
LCC
LCI(G)
PC
PC(S)

8 ⊠ 2
CROWE

8 ⊠ 1
MILLER

2nd
Mar. Div. ⊠ 8
WATSON

N

D-DAY – GREEN BEACH, SAIPAN
15 June 1944, viewed from the west showing the 8th Marines' landing on "Green 1" and "Green 2" and operations inland.

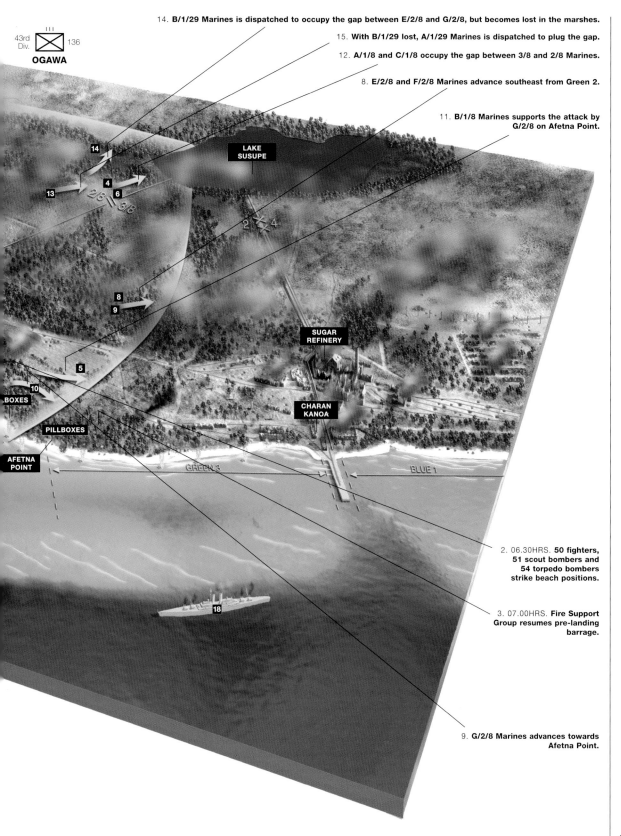

14. **B/1/29 Marines is dispatched to occupy the gap between E/2/8 and G/2/8, but becomes lost in the marshes.**

15. **With B/1/29 lost, A/1/29 Marines is dispatched to plug the gap.**

12. **A/1/8 and C/1/8 occupy the gap between 3/8 and 2/8 Marines.**

8. **E/2/8 and F/2/8 Marines advance southeast from Green 2.**

11. **B/1/8 Marines supports the attack by G/2/8 on Afetna Point.**

43rd Div. 136

OGAWA

LAKE SUSUPE

14

4

13 6

28 3B

2 4

8

9

SUGAR REFINERY

5

10

BOXES

CHARAN KANOA

PILLBOXES

AFETNA POINT

GREEN 3

BLUE 1

2. 06.30HRS. **50 fighters, 51 scout bombers and 54 torpedo bombers strike beach positions.**

3. 07.00HRS. **Fire Support Group resumes pre-landing barrage.**

18

9. **G/2/8 Marines advances towards Afetna Point.**

45

green cane, rains, and light breezes. Most of the Japanese coast defense batteries were knocked out, but not before a battery on Tinian damaged two ships.

At first light on the 14th, frogmen of UDT-5, 6, and 7 reconnoitered the landing beaches, working immediately offshore under the cover of the bombardment. They found no mines or obstacles and were able to blast gaps in the reefs for DUKWs, and chart and mark routes across the reefs with buoys for tanks to wade ashore. UDT-5 and UDT-6 experienced few problems, but UDT-7 on the 4th MarDiv beaches lost four KIA and seven WIA, and only partly completed its mission.

At the same time the 2nd Marines (-), with 1/29 Marines, and 24th Marines, the divisions' reserve regiments, conducted a demonstration off the northwest "Scarlet" and "Black" beaches. Two battleships and a cruiser had been shelling this portion of the coast to reinforce the deception.

D-Day

On the morning of D-Day, 15 June, the reserve regiments conducted a second demonstration off the northwest beaches. Landing craft approached to 5,000yds (4,570m) from shore and circled without receiving fire. The Japanese had in fact determined by 07.30hrs that the UDT activity in the south was on the intended landing beaches. They did retain their units in the north just in case, however, and this prevented them from shifting to the actual landing beaches. The feint also allowed them to claim they had driven off a landing attempt.

Weather conditions were scattered cloud, temperature 83°F (28°C), trade winds light from the northeast, offshore the sea was calm and currents light … for the moment. Smoke from fires partly shrouded the green island. At 05.42hrs H-Hour was designated as 08.30hrs and Adm Turner ordered, "Land the Landing Force." Landing craft were lowered and began the complex assembly process. Thirty-four LSTs carrying the assault troops' amtracs took up station 1,250yds (1,143m) offshore. Behind them were eight LSTs with divisional artillery, two more with AAA units, and two with XXIV Corps Artillery. Their artillery and ammunition were loaded in DUKWs and amtracs. Two landing ships, dock (LSD),

A 27th InfDiv bazooka team prepares to fire on a pillbox on Purple Heart Ridge. The Army used this 2.36in. M9 rocket launcher while the Marines were still armed with the shorter one-piece M1A1.

were in position to launch landing craft, mechanized (LCM), carrying tanks. The transport areas were 18,000yds (16,460m) offshore.

Two battleships, two cruisers, and seven destroyers closed to within 2,500yds (2,286m) offshore firing salvos directly into the beach areas. Ship fire ceased at 06.30hrs and 155 aircraft strafed and bombed the beach areas for 30 minutes. Naval gunfire resumed at 07.00 with such increased intensity that spotters could not adjust fires because of the smoke and dust.

At 07.50 H-Hour was postponed 10 minutes because of difficulties experienced with assembling amtracs after launching. Landing craft, control (LCC), vessels positioned themselves to mark the approach lanes. At 08.12hrs the landing signal was given and 24 landing crafts, infantry (gun) (LCI(G)), advanced ahead of the amtrac waves toward the beaches firing massive 4.5in. rocket barrages. The naval gunfire slackened off by caliber (largest to smallest) as the assault waves approached the beaches. Scores of aircraft strafed, bombed, and rocketed the beaches and then shifted their runs inland as the amtracs closed within 100yds (91m) of the beaches.

The two divisions' assault waves differed in organization. The 2nd MarDiv's first wave for each beach consisted of 12 amtracs in line with a platoon of six amphibian tanks echeloned on each flank and another platoon in the center of the line arranged in a wedge. An LCC or landing craft, vehicle and personnel (LCVP), flanked each wave as guides. The LCI(G)s advanced ahead of the line to halt just short of the reef. Behind the first wave followed the second and third waves with 12 amtracs each and the fourth wave with 14. The 4th MarDiv's first wave consisted of 68 amphibian tanks in line. Behind these were four waves of amtracs.

Enemy fire was light until the LVTs reached the coral reef's lip, at which time artillery, mortar, and machine-gun fire increased drastically. Guide boats were unable to continue past this point. Some control craft had drifted slightly to the north and coupled with a stronger than expected current some 2nd MarDiv units landed north of their intended beaches. The UDTs had not experienced this as the sea conditions and tides were different when they went to work the day before. Once over the reef lip some 400yds (366m) from shore, the swell made station-keeping even more problematic. The swell increased through the day, making unloading and transfer difficult as well as capsizing landing craft and LVTs. The 2nd MarDiv had 31 of its 68 amphibian tanks hit or mechanically disabled before reaching the Tractor Control Line ashore.

In 20 minutes some 8,000 assault troops were ashore. Japanese artillery firing from high ground had sufficient ammunition and would even fire on groups as small as three or four marines. Small groups of Japanese infantry were scattered in-depth through the area hidden in spider holes, rubble, roadside ditches, and camouflaged trenches. Many attempted to infiltrate through gaps between Marine companies with some success.

The 2nd MarDiv's first waves came ashore on the "Red" beaches at 08.40hrs and on the "Green" beaches at 08.43. Most units were some 400yds (366m) too far north with all but 3/8 landing on the beach north of their assigned beach. 2/8 landed on "Green 1" with 3/8, the latter's assigned beach. Most amtracs made it ashore, but troop casualties quickly mounted, especially among leaders. Movement inland was slow. 2/8 was

CLEARING AFETNA POINT, SAIPAN, 16 JUNE 1944
(pages 48–49)

Low rocky Afetna Point separated the 2nd MarDiv's beaches from the 4th MarDiv's to the south. The cruiser USS *Birmingham* (CL-62) stood offshore firing directly into the point and adjacent Japanese positions. 2/8 Marines was to have landed on Beach "Green 2" immediately north of the point. "Green 3" south of the point was left unoccupied while the 4th MarDiv's 3/23 landed on adjacent " Blue 1" to secure the Charan Kanoa pier and its boat channel allowing easy landing of tank-bearing LCMs. Rather than landing on its assigned "Green 2", current and navigation errors caused it to land on "Green 1" to the north along with 3/8 and followed in by the reserve 1/8. With three battalions on one 600yd-wide (548m) beach, congestion and confusion reigned. G/2/8 was assigned the mission of seizing Afetna Point while Companies E and F fanned to the southeast. Landing 700–1,000yds (640–914m) to the north delayed Company G's attack on the point allowing the Japanese to be ready. Nine 37mm and 47mm anti-boat guns in pillboxes (1) covered by rifle trenches were positioned on "Green 2" and the point. Marine regiments had a pool of 100 Winchester 12-gauge M97 trench shotguns (2). All were issued to Company G giving half the men shotguns. The reason for their issue was to provide a short-range weapon to prevent the adjacent 3/23 from being hit by rifle fire. Shot-gunners retained their M1 rifles for later use (3). The shotguns proved effective for close-range antipersonnel use and clearing pillboxes and trenches. The pump-action shotguns held five rounds of 00 buckshot (nine .33-cal lead balls). A problem was encountered with the ammunition. Brass-cased cartridges were not available. Cardboard-cased ammunition (4) was issued and sometimes failed to chamber or extract because of swelling caused by saltwater. M1918A2 BARs (5) provided covering fire for the shot-gunners and engineer demolition men wielding 20lb tetrytol M1 satchel charges (6) attached from C/1/18 Marines. The Japanese gunners often continued to fire on the LCVPs landing follow-on waves as G/2/8 Marines attacked the pillboxes from the rear. The point was cleared with the 2/8 making contact with 1/23 at 11.40hrs, 16 June. (Howard Gerrard)

unable to close the gap that had widened at Afetna Point between 2nd and 4th MarDiv. It was not until D+2 that solid contact was established between the divisions. Inland movement of amtracs was hampered by the unexpected marshes north of Lake Susupe and a 4–5ft (1.2–1.5m) high embankment. 3/8 managed to push inland farther than any other 2nd MarDiv battalion, but was still halted about 900yds (823m) from the O-1 Line. 1/29 came ashore in the late afternoon on the "Green" beaches and was attached to the 8th Marines. The 6th Marines on the north flank experienced the most resistance and was halted by heavy fire from the vicinity of Hill 500 almost 2,000yds (1,829m) from the O-1 Line, which stretched inland farthest from the coast at this point, over 3,000yds (2,743m). Both the 2/6 and 3/6 command posts (CP) were hit by artillery fire resulting in the loss of commanders and key staff. 2/6 had four different battalion commanders on D-Day.

The 4th MarDiv to the south initially lost very few amtracs with 98 percent making it ashore. Only half made it to the Tractor Control Line 500–700yds (457–640m) inland, however. Those amtracs that attempted to advance inland as planned found it hard going. Some amphibian tanks engaged in firefights within Charan Kanoa, which they should have by-passed. Instead, they held up troop-carrying amtracs behind them. Some amtracs managed to pass through regardless of firefights and rubble and advanced on the road heading east to Mt. Fina Susu and the O-1 Line, 1,200–1,500yds (1,097–1,371m) inland. Troops dismounted and dug-in on the feature, but the amphibian tanks remained at the base of the mountain and failed to provide fire support against the Japanese direct-fire weapons blanketing the ridge. Other 23rd Marines elements attempting to pass south of Lake Susupe found impassable marshes. Shell holes, trees, trenches, and rocks halted others. In the south the 25th Marines, finding the terrain impassable to amtracs, dismounted and pushed inland to achieve the O-1 Line, which was closer to the beaches at this point. The Japanese 4th Company, 9th Tank Regiment conducted piecemeal counterattacks on either side of Charan Kanoa with 14 tanks, losing all but three.

A 2nd Marine bazooka team stays on the lookout for targets on the south side of Garapan. It was not until 2 July that the 2nd Marines entered the town, not so much because of resistance, but to wait for units inland, advancing over rough terrain and meeting stiff resistance, to come abreast of them.

By late morning the regimental reserve battalions had landed and by afternoon were in position to support the frontline battalions. Both of the divisional tank battalions were unloaded by late afternoon, but the 4th lost a number of tanks to fire and reef potholes. The 2nd Tank Battalion faired better. Most tanks were sent into the line upon landing, but the 4th held most of its flame-tanks in reserve the first day. The 10th Marines' artillery was unable to begin landing until late afternoon, but by nightfall most howitzers were in action supporting the 2nd MarDiv. The 4th MarDiv's 14th Marines began coming ashore in the early afternoon, but it was early evening before they were in action. The 14th Marines lost a number of howitzers in the surf and others were damaged by enemy fire. Many of these were later repaired and returned to action. Both the divisions' reserve regiments began landing in the early afternoon, but it was near nightfall before all were ashore and in position. The 24th Marines suffered almost 400 casualties in the process from LVT accidents and artillery fire. At 19.00hrs the order was given that no more troops would be landed that day. Only the 1st and 3rd Battalions of 2nd Marines had landed.

Over 2,000 casualties were suffered on D-Day. In the confusion, no accurate determination could be made of dead and wounded, combat and accidental deaths. Many wounded were treated and retuned to duty and others were not treated until the next day or days later. Artillery and mortar fire had taken the heaviest toll, followed by machine-gun and rifle fire, and then edged weapons in the hand-to-hand combat ashore. Drownings and capsized landing craft and LVTs accounted for numerous deaths. The three hospital LSTs, to which 40 percent of the casualties were sent, proved unsatisfactory as they were soon filled to capacity with 200 casualties each. The wounded had to be transferred to transports, causing them more discomfort.

Navy beach parties and Marine shore parties came ashore in the early afternoon. Cooperation between the elements was excellent. Little cargo-handling equipment could be landed the first day, and this, coupled with

27th InfDiv troops prepare to advance toward Hill 767, a point near the upper northwest coast above Paradise Valley, the last Japanese CP. 1/25 Marines would secure the hill on 4 July. A Japanese 20mm Type 98 (1938) automatic cannon sits abandoned in the photograph's center.

the increasingly difficult surf conditions, hampered supplies and equipment unloading. Few units experienced shortages, however, as amtracs in the second, third, and fourth waves carried additional small arms and mortar ammunition, grenades, and water to be off-loaded on the beach. Additionally, each battalion had two amtracs loaded with the same, along with rations and medical supplies. These came ashore after the initial landing and carried the supplies inland to the unit.

By nightfall only the 25th Marines on the south flank had reached the O-1 Line. Only parts of three 23rd Marines companies made it to the O-1 Line near Mt. Fina Susu. The 4th MarDiv wisely withdrew these exposed, understrength units 800yds (732m) west to the main line. The two divisions held a 10,000yd (9,144m) front stretching 1,500yds (1,371m) inland at its deepest. It enclosed less than half the planned beachhead – the O-1 Line. Efforts were being made to sort out scattered units, link up flanks, register artillery fire, and move critical supplies forward. Afetna Point, though partly cleared, was still held by the Japanese and separated the two divisions, each of which refused their flanks creating a 400–500yd (365–457m) "channel" between them leading to Afetna Point. While having taken less than one-third of the O-1 Line, still largely on low ground, the troops were in good shape and were there to stay. The Japanese 136th Infantry facing the 2nd MarDiv and 47th IMB facing the 4th MarDiv still held the high ground, however, and had adequate artillery. The Marines dug in and prepared for a long night.

Probes and small counterattacks lasted through the night but were easily defeated. The 6th Marines experienced a major attack at 03.00hrs, however. A minor penetration was achieved, although erroneous reports to the regimental CP indicated a worse situation and a tank platoon was committed. This broke the Japanese attack and at dawn over 700 Japanese dead were found. They were from a 135th Infantry battalion sent down from the Northern Sector. Some small groups had infiltrated into the rear, but were mopped up in the morning. As these units withdrew the Yokosuka 1st SNLF, sent south from the Naval Sector, mistook them for Americans and a sharp firefight broke out between

IJN and IJA troops. In the 4th MarDiv sector the 25th Marines experienced two counterattacks. The 04.30hrs attack was preceded by an artillery preparation with the Japanese forcing women and children ahead of them as a ruse. With extremely effective Marine artillery support the attack was beaten back. Japanese artillery struck a Marine 75mm gun halftrack and it burned so brightly that one company was forced to withdraw 200yds (182m) as the fire silhouetted their position for Japanese observers. They reoccupied their position at dawn. The 23rd Marines on the left contended with repeated small attacks and infiltrations through the night originating from the gap between them and the 2nd MarDiv to the north. The final attack occurred at 05.30hrs out of the Lake Susupe area toward the Charan Kanoa pier and the 200 attackers were wiped out.

Securing the South (D+1 to D+6)

On D+1 (16 June) the first order of business was to consolidate the beachhead and close the gap at Afetna Point between the two divisions. 2/8 Marines accomplished this by 12.00hrs. On the north flank the 6th Marines made no advances, but prepared for further counterattacks. The 4th MarDiv advanced with its three regiments in line toward Fina Susu Ridge. On its north flank the 23rd Marines made little headway because of strong resistance on Mt. Fina Susu itself and the marshes south of Lake Susupe. The 8th Marines north of the lake were slowed by marshes as well. The 24th Marines in the center pushed close to the O-1 Line, while on the south flank the 25th Marines secured Agingan Point on the south edge of " Yellow 3" and drove beyond the O-1 Line. However, strong resistance halted the regiment as it approached Aslito Airfield. By dark the advance parties of all XXIV Corps Artillery units were ashore, but no artillery. It was decided to postpone the Guam landing scheduled for 18 June to an unspecified date. This was not due to a slower than anticipated advance as sometimes stated, but because of the movement of the Combined Fleet through San Bernardino Strait in the Philippines, the first moves of Operation *A-Go*.

The Japanese 136th Infantry and 9th Tank Regiments were to counterattack the center of the 2nd MarDiv sector at 17.00hrs. Yokosuka 1st SNLF was to attack the north flank. The units were still disorganized from the previous night's action and the attack was not launched until 03.30hrs. An estimated 37 tanks and some 500 infantry hit mainly 1/6 and 2/2 Marines. Marine tanks, anti-tank guns, bazookas, and artillery destroyed at least 24 tanks and 300 infantry. The attack, the largest tank battle in the Pacific Theater, was broken off at 07.00 with about 100 Marine casualties.

On 16 June other Japanese island commanders were ordered to send reinforcements to Saipan. Tinian was unable to send I/135 as the narrow Saipan Straits was heavily patrolled. The 52nd Division at Truk was to send two battalions, but they had no craft available. On the night of 21 June, Guam dispatched two companies reinforced by artillery aboard 13 barges, rather than the ordered battalion, but heavy seas prevented them from going any further than Rota.

The 27th InfDiv (less 106th Infantry), 30 miles (48km) from Saipan, was notified it would immediately land over the 4th MarDiv beaches. 1st and 2nd Battalions, 165th Infantry came ashore over "Blue 1" in the early hours of the morning and was attached to the 4th MarDiv. It moved inland through 3/24, took up position on the 4th MarDiv's south flank, and prepared to attack toward Aslito Airfield at 07.30hrs. Most of the 27th InfDiv artillery was landed on the morning of the 17th.

D+2 saw the 2nd MarDiv attack to almost double its beachhead area. The 2nd Marines pushed north with 3/2 and 2/6 to within 1,000yds (914m) of Garapan. The 6th Marines secured the base of Mt. Tipo Pale with 1/6, 3/6, and 2/2 in the line. The 8th Marines moved around Lake Susupe with 1/8, 3/8, and 1/29, the latter having difficulties in the swamps. As the advance progressed, another gap developed between the divisions. 2/8 refused its south flank to cover the gap. 1/2 was the Division Reserve.

The 4th MarDiv attack made even better headway advancing beyond the ridge, although the 23rd Marines were slowed south of Lake Susupe's swamps and soon ground to a halt with 1/23, 3/23, and 2/23 in the line.

The aftermath of the 7 July *gyokysai* destruction attack left scores of dead Japanese on the beach in the 2/105 Infantry's area. In the far distance are Marine Sherman tanks participating in the 6th Marines' mopping-up.

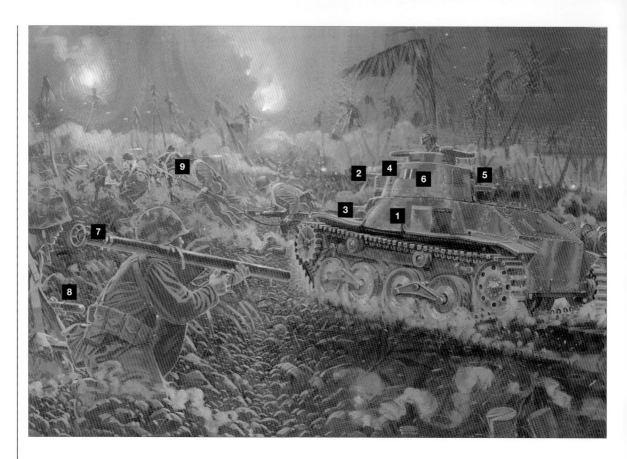

JAPANESE TANK ATTACK, SAIPAN, 16 JUNE 1944
(pages 56–57)

On 16 June Col Ogawa of the 136th Infantry Regiment, Col Goto of the 9th Tank Regiment, and LtCdr Karashima of the Yokosuka 1st SNLF received orders to attack toward the radio station off the northeast of end of the Charan Kanoa Airstrip, now in American hands. Realistically LtGen Saito expected the attack only to succeed in penetrating to a point 400yds (366m) within the Marine line, but still 500–600yds (457–549m) from the water's edge. He would then use it as a position to drive a wedge into the 2nd MarDiv's beachhead on the boundary line separating the 6th and 8th Marines. This counterattack should have been launched the night before when the Marines were not so far inland or as strong ashore. The attack was launched at 03.30hrs hitting 1/6 Marines and F/2/2 with some 1,000 infantry and approximately 37 of the remaining 44 tanks making it the largest tank battle in the Pacific. The 9th Tank Regiment (-) had three medium and three light tanks in the headquarters and 11 mediums and three lights in its companies with two mediums and three lights, for reconnaissance, in the company headquarters and three mediums in each of the three platoons. At the time of the counterattack the 3rd and 5th Companies were at full strength as was the battalion headquarters. Only three survived from the 4th Company's D-Day actions and the 6th Company had seven. The medium

tanks were the 57mm gun-armed Type 97 (1937) *Chi-Ha* while the 12 lights were the Type 95 (1935) *Ha-Go*. The 7.4-ton Type 95 (1) tank had a 110 horsepower diesel engine and its armor was 6–12mm. It was armed with a 37mm gun Type 97 (1937) gun (2) for which 130 rounds of high explosive and armor-piercing ammunition was carried. The driver sat on the right and to his left was a gunner for the bow 7.7mm Type 97 (1937) machine-gun (3) with 1,170 rounds of ammunition. A pistol port was fitted in either side of his compartment with another in the left front quarter of the turret (4). In the 5 o'clock rear turret position was another 7.7mm machine gun (5) with 1,800 rounds. Its odd positioning was because of space limitations. The tank commander manned the one-man turret to double as the gunner. The green and white symbol on the turret side (6) identifies this tank as belonging to the Regiment's 3rd Company. Both medium and light Japanese tanks were easily knocked out by US 75mm guns aboard tanks and half-tracks, 37mm AT guns, and 2.36in. bazookas. The M1A1 bazooka (7) weighed 13.2lbs and had an effective range of 250yds (229m). The M6A3 high explosive antitank rocket (8) could penetrate 4–5 inches (100–130mm) of armor with three carried in an M6 bag. Japanese infantrymen riding into action aboard the tanks quickly dismounted when engaged (9), but nevertheless some 300 were cut down and at least 24 tanks were destroyed. (Howard Gerrard)

One of the few remaining Japanese Type 95 (1935) *Ha-Go* 37mm light tanks was knocked out by the 105th Infantry during the *gyokusai* attack, what the 27th InfDiv simply called "The Raid".

The 24th Marines had received heavy artillery, mortar, and direct AA fire during their attack, but were able to gain the ridge with 2/24 and 1/24. 3/24 was the Division Reserve. The 25th Marines gained the northwest edge of Aslito Airfield and had to place all three battalions (1/25, 2/25, and 3/25) in the line, but a gap still existed between the 25th Marines and 165th Infantry. The 165th advanced toward the airfield with 2/165 and 1/165. 1/165 sealed off a pocket of Japanese on Cape Obiam on its right. 3/165 came ashore later as did the 105th Infantry and Division HQ. NTLF HQ came ashore as well.

At 04.30hrs on 18 June, Japanese I/18 Infantry attempted to conduct a counter-landing on the Marine beachhead sailing from Tanapag Harbor in 35 barges. LCI gunboats interdicted the force and, with the help of Marine artillery, destroyed many of the craft and drove off the rest.

D+3 saw the 2nd and 4th MarDivs attack at 10.00hrs. The 27th InfDiv launched its attack at 12.00hrs as it needed time to deploy the 105th Infantry. The 2nd MarDiv made only slight advances of no more than 100–300yds (91–274m) against the resolute defenders. The 4th MarDiv made good headway with the 23rd Marines finally fighting its way out of the swamps, but another gap was created between the divisions. The 24th Marines reached the base of Hill 500 and the 25th Marines made it to Magicienne Bay cutting the island in two. The 27th InfDiv overran the airfield [5] with the 165th and the 105th clearing Cape Obiam and the ground south of the airfield. Numerous Japanese were now cut off from the north on Nafutan Point. Prime Minister Tojo radioed the garrison with a rather fatalistic message, "Have received your honorable Imperial words. By becoming the bulwark of the Pacific with 10,000 deaths; we hope to acquire Imperial favor."

On D+4 the 2nd MarDiv only probed and sent out patrols. They were waiting for the 4th MarDiv to clear the south and then move north to come into the line to the east of the 2nd MarDiv. The 4th MarDiv launched its attack after breaking up assembling enemy troops near Tsutsuran Village with the 23rd Marines, 3/24 attached, advancing almost to Hill 500. They were forced to withdraw some 400yds (364m), however, as their flank was exposed. The other two regiments only consolidated their positions. The 27th InfDiv attack ran into problems as the two regiments separated creating a gap. The 165th was stretched thin as it maintained contact with the 4th MarDiv and the 105th Infantry. The latter was confronted with rough terrain and steep cliffs. 1/165, the Regimental Reserve, had to fill the gap. Overall there were few gains 19 June. The Japanese had, however, suffered major losses by this time. The 43rd Division had lost $3^{1}/_{2}$ of it its seven battalions and two-thirds of its artillery. The 47th IMB had lost all of its artillery and could not determine what infantry was still capable of fighting. Two of the three straggler battalions had been lost as had three engineer companies and all but one AAA battery. The remnants had begun to withdraw to a defensive line running from just south of Garapan to Mt. Tipo Pale and then southeast to Magicienne Bay just north of Tsutsuran. The 4th MarDiv adjusted its regiments as it pivoted north with the 23rd now in reserve, the 25th on the left, and the 24th on the right.

D+5, 20 June, saw the 2nd Marines advance to just south of Garapan. The 6th Marines could advance no further, even pulling back their center around 200 yards (183m), until the 8th Marines secured Hill 500. Further advance by the 6th would have exposed their flank to the enemy on the hill. The capture of this feature was pivotal to the Division's turning movement. 2/8 advanced to the left of Hill 500 resulting in a shortening of the lines enabling 3/8 and 1/29 to be pulled back into reserve. 1/8 and 2/8 assaulted at 09.00hrs with massive fire support and soon secured the hill with light casualties. The 25th Marines also advanced toward Hill 500 and would relieve the 8th Marines there. The 24th Marine rushed forward 2,700 yards (2,468m) toward Tsutsuran. The 27th InfDiv made little headway in the south pushing the Japanese on to the more rugged ground of Nafutan Point. The 106th Infantry came ashore in the morning and was assigned as the NTLF Reserve.

D+6 saw both Marine divisions reorganizing, resupplying, and probing in preparation for the push north. Japanese hidden in the Lake Susupe swamps were rooted out. From left to right the regiments in the line were 2nd, 6th, 8th, 25th, and 24th with the divisions' boundary running north up the central ridge and hill mass and bending east around Mt. Tapotchau so that the feature was within the 2nd MarDiv's

A Marine M1A1 flamethrower burns out a cave hidden behind a house in Paradise Valley on the northwest coast. The Japanese referred to the area, where their late CP was located, as Valley of Hell.

The 24th Marines captured the Marpi Point Airstrip on 9 July. The Japanese had continued to work on the airstrip on the island's extreme north end in expectation of air reinforcement from Japan.

zone. The 27th InfDiv had to fight its way slowly through every cave and ravine on Nafutan Point. NTLF ordered the Division to leave only one battalion to mop up the point and for the rest to assemble northwest of the airfield as the NTLF Reserve to support the advance north. The division commander requested that a regiment be allowed to complete the task. NTLF agreed, but the regiment's reserve 2/105 would be available for operations elsewhere, pending the division commander's approval for release. The 105th would take over the mission.

Battle of the Philippine Sea, 19–20 June

The 1st Mobile Fleet, designated the 1st Mobile Force for Operation *A-Go*, under Vice Adm Ozawa Jisaburo, had departed Tawitawi on 13 June. This Force contained 90 percent of the Combined Fleet, the IJN's surface striking force. It was preparing to launch Operation *Kon*, the reinforcement of Biak, but the discovery of the US fleet heading for the Marianas forced implementation of *A-Go*. The Force consisted of nine carriers with 473 aircraft, five battleships, 13 cruisers, 28 destroyers, and seven oilers backed by 24 submarines. The Force steamed through San Bernardino Strait between Samar and Luzon with US submarines reporting its progress. The Force refueled on 17 June and hoped the US carriers would proceed toward Yap or the Palaus as Japanese fuel was dwindling. On the 18th Japanese land-based bombers attacked the US fleet off Saipan inflicting little damage. Virtually all of the aircraft sent to the island from Japan were lost in air battles or on the ground with minimal US losses. Between the 15th and 18th both forces sought to locate the other with submarines and patrol aircraft.

On the morning of the 19th the 1st Mobile Force launched the first of its four large air attacks against TF 58 some 200 miles (322km) west of Saipan. The two forces were about 100 nautical miles (185km) apart. The Battle of the Philippine Sea, or what the Japanese called the Battle for the Marianas, had begun. TF 58 had 15 carriers with 956 aircraft, seven battleships, 21 cruisers, 69 destroyers, and 25 submarines. US aircraft intercepted all four raids inflicting massive losses on the Japanese with little damage suffered by TF 58. US aircraft also destroyed most of the

Beach "White 1" on Tinian was 60yds wide with a 200yd-wide approach across the 50yd-wide reef. In this low-tide photograph coral outcroppings and ledges can be seen on the beach. Brush and trees can be seen behind the beach. Note the power line along the road leading to the left. The dark horizontal lines in the distance are aircraft revetments around Airfield No. 1.

Japanese aircraft on Guam losing only 30 aircraft. American submarines sank two Japanese carriers. The Japanese changed course and TF 58 was unable to deliver its own attack until the evening of 20 June, sinking one carrier and damaging two. Because of the range some 80 US aircraft were forced to ditch at sea or crashed on the carrier deck upon return. Only 20 were lost to enemy action.

The battered 1st Mobile Force withdrew northwestward with TF 58 making only a halfhearted effort to pursue. Instead, it refueled and returned to Saipan. The "Great Marianas Turkey Shoot" was over. Only one US battleship and one cruiser were slightly damaged and 130 aircraft lost, most as a result of non-combat causes. The 1st Mobile Force limped into Okinawa with some ships proceeding to Japan for repairs. Japanese losses were three carriers sunk, three damaged (one heavily), one battleship, cruiser, and destroyer damaged, and two oilers sunk. The irreparable damage though was the loss of 476 aircraft and 445 aviators, both carrier and shore based. Only 35 carrier aircraft were operational. Adm Ozawa tendered his resignation, but it was refused. He retained his command, but lost his remaining carriers off Leyte during the October 1944 Battle of Cape Engano.

Seizing Central Saipan (D+7 to D+11)

The attack into the rugged central Saipan hills was scheduled to launch at 06.00hrs, 22 June (D+7). To this point the 2nd MarDiv had suffered 2,514 casualties, 4th MarDiv 3,628, and 27th InfDiv 320. The 2nd MarDiv at the foot of Mt. Tipo Pale would seize the hill and take Mt. Tapotchau 3,000yds (2,743m) in front of them. The 4th MarDiv would move up the inland road to secure a valley and ridge to the southeast of Mt. Tapotchau and take Hill 600 just north of Magicienne Bay. The 27th InfDiv (less the 105th Infantry Regiment) was to be prepared to support either Marine division if either became overextended.

Eighteen artillery battalions supported the attack. The 2nd Marines remained in place on the coast while 3/6 easily secured Mt. Tipo Pale, although a strongpoint at its base held out for two days. The 8th Marines covered the most ground, but were finally halted southeast of Mt. Tipo Pale. The 25th Marines attacked in a column of battalions securing three small ridgelines before being halted at the fourth. Nevertheless, they advanced some 2,000yds (1,829m). The 24th Marines advanced along the shore of the bay, hampered by ravines perpendicular to their route. As their front widened, the reserve 23rd Marines were plugged into the line between the 25th and 24th. This reduced the 24th's front and it attacked in a column of battalions. It was halted 200 yards (183m) from Hill 600. During the night the 27th InfDiv began to relieve the 25th Marines, which was placed in NTLF Reserve. The 23rd and 24th Marines would continue to advance around the north shore of Magicienne Bay and clear Kagman Peninsula. The 27th InfDiv would clear the eastern slopes of Mt. Tapotchau with the 106th Infantry, and the 165th Infantry would advance up the valley road and the ridge that ran parallel, what would become known as Death Valley and Purple Heart Ridge. The 105th Infantry on Nafutan Point became the NTLF Reserve and its 2/105 would continue to clear the point including 407ft (124m) Mt. Nafutan.

The D+8 attack was a continuation of the previous day's assault. Enemy resistance increased, however, and few gains were made. On the coast 2/2 was pinched out of the line allowing 2/6 to be returned to its parent regiment. A gap developed between 6th and 8th Marines, however, with the 6th Marines held up clearing pockets of resistance on Mt. Tipo Pale. The 8th Marines initially met little resistance moving toward Mt. Tapotchau, but were halted as the 106th Infantry on their right had not yet advanced. 2/8 protected the flank and the rest of the Regiment advanced securing the cliffs in front of Mt. Tapotchau. F/2/106 was attached to the 8th in an effort to maintain contact. The 27th InfDiv attack was delayed as units became intermixed as they moved into position over the rough terrain. They attacked between 10.00 and 11.00hrs and the 106th ran into a strongpoint dubbed Hell's Pocket, while the 165th was halted by strong positions on Purple Heart Ridge. The 23rd Marines secured Hill 600 as the 24th reached Laulau Village. Hill 600 gave the Marines unobstructed observation of Kagman Peninsula and Laulau was its gateway. An afternoon enemy counterattack saw five tanks and infantry attempt to penetrate the line at the Marine and Army boundary, and another five tanks hit the 106th.

The remains of an LVT(2) destroyed by a horned anti-boat mine on "White 2". Mines also destroyed two other amtracs. Although 100 mines were found on the beach, most had deteriorated or were unarmed. The amtrac's bow is to the left. The mine detonated beneath the driver's compartment.

Four battalions of 75mm M1A1 pack howitzers were landed on Tinian on J-Day to provide close-in fire support. Thirteen 105mm howitzer, 155mm howitzer, and 155mm gun battalions provided long-range fires from the south end of Saipan.

The 23rd Marines beat off an attack on Hill 600. LtGen Smith was highly displeased with the 27th InfDiv's failure to advance and the division commander's perceived lack of will. He discussed this with MajGen Jarman, the senior Army officer on Saipan and Garrison Force commander. Jarman explained the situation to MajGen Smith, who was already expecting to be relieved. Smith assured Jarman he would personally see to it that the assault regiments advanced on time the next day. The reality was that the terrain in the 27th InfDiv's zone was much rougher than the Marines' and the resistance stronger.

The D+9 objectives were Mt. Tapotchau, Death Valley, Purple Heart Ridge, and Kagman Peninsula. The 2nd Marines attacked toward Garapan and beat off two enemy counterattacks, one involving seven tanks of which only one escaped. The Provisional Battalion, 2nd MarDiv was organized with five companies from shore party personnel and sent to support 2/2. The 27th InfDiv in the center ran into extremely tough resistance and difficult terrain. The 106th Infantry could not reduce Hell's Pocket and fell back to its start line while the 165th made no headway into Death Valley or on Purple Heart Ridge. The 4th MarDiv pivoted on to the Kagman Peninsula securing about one-third of it.

LtGen Smith was furious with the 27th InfDiv's failures, accusing the Army troops of being unwilling to fight. He relieved MajGen Smith at 17.00hrs and put MajGen Jarman in command. Smith offered to stay with Jarman until the next morning to ensure he was familiar with on-going operations. NTLF agreed to this, but then LtGen Smith ordered MajGen Smith off the island and he was flown to Eniwetok at 05.00hrs. Jarman did his best to get the Division moving, but with little success.[6]

On D+10 (25 June) the 2nd Marines held fast outside Garapan while 1/29 and 2/8 attacked Mt. Tapotchau. The commander of 1/29 led a 2nd Reconnaissance Company detachment to the crest and returned to his battalion to bring two companies up. They had to beat back several counterattacks, but the Marines retained the highest point on the island. The 27th InfDiv was still having trouble and making no progress. Although 2/165 had gained one-third of Purple Heart Ridge and 2/106 had penetrated well into Death Valley, they withdrew to better night defensive positions. Most of the 106th had pulled completely out of its zone leaving a gap with 2/106 and 3/106 now in the 165th's sector and 1/106, 3/165,

and 1/105 now on the 4th MarDiv's north flank digging in along the division boundary facing west. These moves were an unsuccessful effort to outflank Purple Heart Ridge and seal off Death Valley. The 4th MarDiv made good headway on Kagman Peninsula and it was apparent that organized resistance there was nearing an end. That night the Japanese sent a company from Tinian in 11 barges. Discovered off the east coast by destroyers, one was sunk and the remainder fled.

During this period the Japanese 43rd Division had faced the 2nd MarDiv and 27th InfDiv while the Japanese 47th IMB and other units faced the 4th MarDiv. They had ceased to function as cohesive formations and were now only loose collections of scattered elements. 31st Army could account for only 950 combatants. Other scattered elements totaling at least 2,000–3,000, although having lost touch with their parent formation, were still fighting. These included 500 47th IMB troops and stragglers on Nafutan Point. All artillery had been destroyed and only three tanks remained. From this point on the Japanese began experiencing increasingly severe water shortages. LtGen Saito sent a message to Tokyo, "Please apologize deeply to the Emperor that we cannot do better than we are."

On D+11 (26 June) the 6th Marines bypassed the strongpoints holding them up around Mt. Tipo Pale and secured the ridge connecting it to Mt. Tapotchau. The 8th Marines extended its line to the rear to cover the gap left by the 106th, but was unable to make contact. 1/106 continued to try to reduce Hell's Pocket while the other two battalions attacked the west side of Purple Heart Ridge. The attack got off to a confused start, resulting in MajGen Jarman relieving Colonel Russell G. Ayers. The 4th MarDiv on Kagman Peninsula were now pinched out of the line and became the NTLF Reserve. The Division was ordered to prepare to reenter the lines that evening, less the 25th Marines but with the 165th Infantry attached. That night the holdouts on Nafutan Point infiltrated through 2/105 lines suffering losses and attacked the 25th Marines on Hill 500 where they were wiped out. The wounded left on the point had committed suicide. 2/105 finished clearing the little remaining resistance on 27 June.

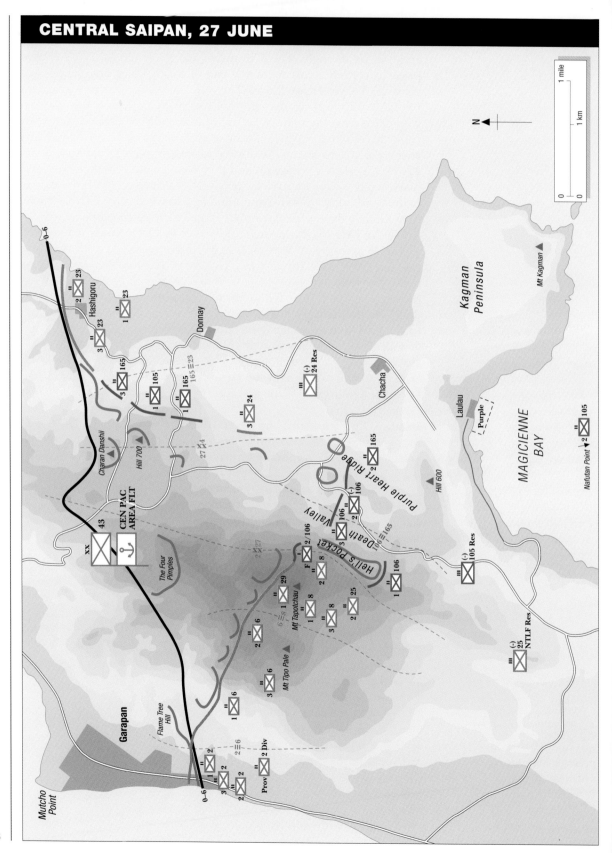

The Push North (D+12 to D+19)

On D+12 (27 June) the 2nd MarDiv readjusted its lines and made some advances on the right. The 27th InfDiv finally surrounded Hell's Pocket, placed a cordon across the north end of Death Valley, and made some gains on Purple Heart Ridge. The 4th MarDiv pushed well ahead of the 27th InfDiv along the east coast with the 165th on the left and 23rd Marines on the right. 3/24 had to secure the gap created on the left flank ahead of the 27th. The Japanese were preparing a final defense line anchored on Tanapag on the northwest coast through Tarahoho and Hill 221 on the island's centerline and then southeastward to the coast. This line roughly followed a road running across the island. The headquarters of the Northern Marianas Army Group (43rd Division) and Central Pacific Area Fleet finally occupied the same location and essentially merged.

The 2nd MarDiv made some headway on D+13 and finally reduced the Tipo Pale strongpoint. MajGen George W. Griner arrived from Hawaii to take over the 27th InfDiv from Jarman at 10.30hrs. He immediately realigned units and the 105th Infantry was placed in the line to the right of the 106th. The 27th InfDiv only had four battalions under its direct control during this period: 106th Infantry and 3/105. The 165th, with 1/105, remained attached to the 4th MarDiv. 2/105 was still on Nafutan Point. The 4th MarDiv slowed its advance as it had pushed well ahead of the 27th InfDiv.

Over the next two days the Marine divisions virtually halted as a result of fatigue and the need for the 27th InfDiv to catch up with their advance. During the 29th and 30th the 27th InfDiv finally managed to overrun Death Valley, Purple Heart Ridge, and Hell's Pocket. The Division had accomplished an extremely tough assignment and had lost some 1,400 men in the weeklong struggle. The Japanese began withdrawing to their final defensive line on the night of D+15.

D+16 (1 July) again saw little advance as pockets were cleared out. However, patrols found little opposition to their front. On D+17 (2 July) the 2nd MarDiv attacked Garapan, but the final pocket in the town was not reduced until 4 July. The 165th Infantry was returned to 27th InfDiv

The Japanese also lost five of the 12 Type 95 (1935) *Ha-Go* light tanks belonging to Tank Company, 18th Infantry Regiment during the 24/25 July counterattacks. These tanks were knocked out by a barrage of Marine 75mm guns mounted on Shermans and halftracks, 37mm AT guns, and bazookas.

control on 1 July, and the Division made gains of up to 1,800 yards (1,645m). From 1 to 4 July the 2nd MarDiv reached Flores Point north of Garapan, the 27th InfDiv seized the west anchor of the new Japanese defense line, Tanapag, and the 4th MarDiv took Hill 221, the Japanese line's center, and easily penetrated much of the rest of the line. The 23rd Marines were stretched across half the width of the island, at this point 4,000yds (3,657m) wide, while the 24th and 25th Marines reached the northwest coast. The latter had been released from the NTLF Reserve on 3 July. That night the 2nd MarDiv was pulled out of the line and became the NTLF Reserve.

The Last Battles (D+20 to D+24)

On D+20 (5 July) the 27th InfDiv took over the west of the line with the 105th on the left and the 165th on the right. Rough terrain and stiff resistance slowed it. The 4th MarDiv advanced further up the east side of the narrowing island with the 24th and 25th Marines in the line. On D+21 the 2nd Marines was attached to the 4th MarDiv and inserted between the 23rd and 24th Marines. The 27th InfDiv was having particular trouble reducing areas known as the Coconut Grove and Hara-kiri Gulch near Tanapag Village.

LtGen Saito's CP was now in small valley near Makunsha Village on the northwest coast, dubbed Paradise Valley by the Americans and Valley of Hell by the Japanese. Before dawn on 7 July, Saito ordered a final *banzai* attack on the 27th InfDiv. It is reported to have actually been a *gyokysai*[7]. The attack's unrealistic goal was to fight through Garapan, Charan Kanoa, and then across the island to Nafutan Point, where it was thought that 47th IMB troops were still holding out. Saito also told the troops that a Japanese landing force was en route from Japan and that troops would be airlifted into the Marpi Point airfield, on which work was continued. Such an effort was actually planned, but abandoned when it was realized that American sea and air power made it unfeasible. The Japanese attack, what the 27th InfDiv simply called "The Raid", was launched at 04.00hrs by an estimated 3,000 troops from all units. 1st and 2nd Battalions, 105th Infantry and 3/10 Marines [artillery] (attached to the 4th MarDiv) were overrun and the survivors pushed back over 1,000 yds to Tanapag. The attack began to run down at 11.30hrs though fighting continued all day. Saito committed suicide that morning. The lost ground was regained by 18.00hrs. Including Japanese killed earlier by artillery and naval gunfire, 4,311 dead were found in the area. The 105th Infantry lost 406 killed in action (KIA) and 512 wounded in action (WIA). 3/10 Marines lost 45 KIA and 82 WIA. The two already under-strength Army battalions were now combat ineffective. Little Japanese organized resistance remained after the *gyokysai*.

On the night of 7 July the 2nd MarDiv relieved most of the Army units, moving into the line with the 6th and 8th Marines and 165th Infantry facing northwest toward the narrow coastal strip. The 4th MarDiv also pushed toward the northwest coast with the 23rd, 2nd, and 24th Marines as the 25th pushed north. The 23rd was pinched out of the line on 8 July as the coast was reached. On the 9th the 2nd Marines secured Mt. Marpi as the 24th took the airstrip and reached Marpi Point. The 25th Marines cleared the east portion of the island's northeast end. Vice Adm Turner declared Saipan secure at 16.15hrs and MajGen Jarman's Garrison Force took control of the island.

On Tinian a steady stream of amtracs and Ducks flowed ashore bring in support troops, ammunition, water, rations, and other supplies. The consolidated NTLF and 4th MarDiv Shore Party also supported the 2nd MarDiv relieving it of shore party responsibilities.

A final horror experienced on Saipan was the mass suicide of hundreds of Japanese civilians – men, women, and children. Many threw themselves and their children off the island's northern cliffs. The Americans attempted to stop them using loudspeakers and Japanese-American linguists, but often to no avail.

Mopping-up was to continue for sometime. On 13 July 3/6 Marines assaulted Maniagassa Island in Tanapag Harbor using LVTs. The garrison's three 120mm guns had long since been knocked out. Five Japanese and 10 Korean laborers were taken prisoner and 16 Japanese killed with one Marine WIA. This was the end of Marine operations on Saipan as they prepared for Tinian.

The 105th Infantry was placed under the control of the Garrison Force. 27th InfDiv Artillery was attached to XXIV Corps Artillery to support the Tinian assault on 15 July. The remainder of the 27th InfDiv was designated the NTLF Reserve for possible use on Tinian. The Division was then attached to the Garrison Force and a major sweep of Saipan was made with all three regiments in line starting north of Tanapag Harbor and moving north culminating on 5 August.

The 105th Infantry departed for Espíritu Santo in mid-August. The last 27th InfDiv element departed on 4 October. It would see its last battle on Okinawa. XXIV Corps Artillery departed for Hawaii in August and would relieve VAC Artillery on Leyte in December.

5 Aslito Airfield was renamed Conroy Field after Col Gardiner J. Conroy, CO, 165th Infantry, killed on Makin.
6 The Buckner Board, the formal Army investigation, concluded that LtGen Smith 1) had full authority to relieve MajGen Smith, 2) the change of command order was properly issued, 3) LtGen Smith was not fully informed of the 27th InfDiv's station and conditions, and 4) the relief of MajGen Smith "was not justified by the facts."
7 A *gyokysai* (lit.– breaking the jewel) can only be ordered by the Emperor and obligates units to utterly destroy themselves in a final devastating attack. It has never been confirmed whether this was actually ordered by the Emperor or if the troops were simply told that by Saito.

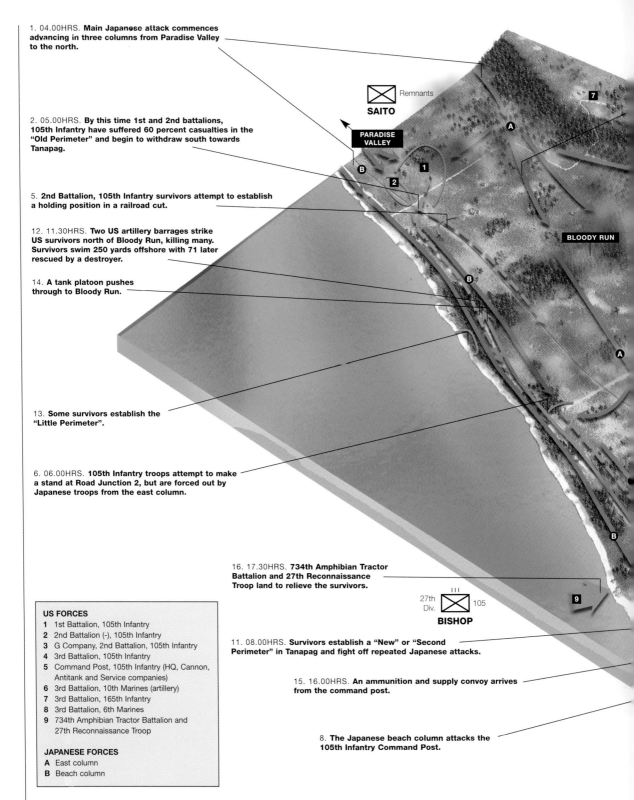

1. 04.00HRS. **Main Japanese attack commences advancing in three columns from Paradise Valley to the north.**

2. 05.00HRS. **By this time 1st and 2nd battalions, 105th Infantry have suffered 60 percent casualties in the "Old Perimeter" and begin to withdraw south towards Tanapag.**

5. **2nd Battalion, 105th Infantry survivors attempt to establish a holding position in a railroad cut.**

12. 11.30HRS. **Two US artillery barrages strike US survivors north of Bloody Run, killing many. Survivors swim 250 yards offshore with 71 later rescued by a destroyer.**

14. **A tank platoon pushes through to Bloody Run.**

13. **Some survivors establish the "Little Perimeter".**

6. 06.00HRS. **105th Infantry troops attempt to make a stand at Road Junction 2, but are forced out by Japanese troops from the east column.**

16. 17.30HRS. **734th Amphibian Tractor Battalion and 27th Reconnaissance Troop land to relieve the survivors.**

11. 08.00HRS. **Survivors establish a "New" or "Second Perimeter" in Tanapag and fight off repeated Japanese attacks.**

15. 16.00HRS. **An ammunition and supply convoy arrives from the command post.**

8. **The Japanese beach column attacks the 105th Infantry Command Post.**

SAITO — Remnants

PARADISE VALLEY

BLOODY RUN

27th Div. — 105 — BISHOP

US FORCES

1 1st Battalion, 105th Infantry
2 2nd Battalion (-), 105th Infantry
3 G Company, 2nd Battalion, 105th Infantry
4 3rd Battalion, 105th Infantry
5 Command Post, 105th Infantry (HQ, Cannon, Antitank and Service companies)
6 3rd Battalion, 10th Marines (artillery)
7 3rd Battalion, 165th Infantry
8 3rd Battalion, 6th Marines
9 734th Amphibian Tractor Battalion and 27th Reconnaissance Troop

JAPANESE FORCES

A East column
B Beach column

JAPANESE *BANZAI* ATTACK

Night of 6/7 July 1944, viewed from the southwest, showing the massed attack by the final remnants of Saipan's defenders on the 105th Infantry.

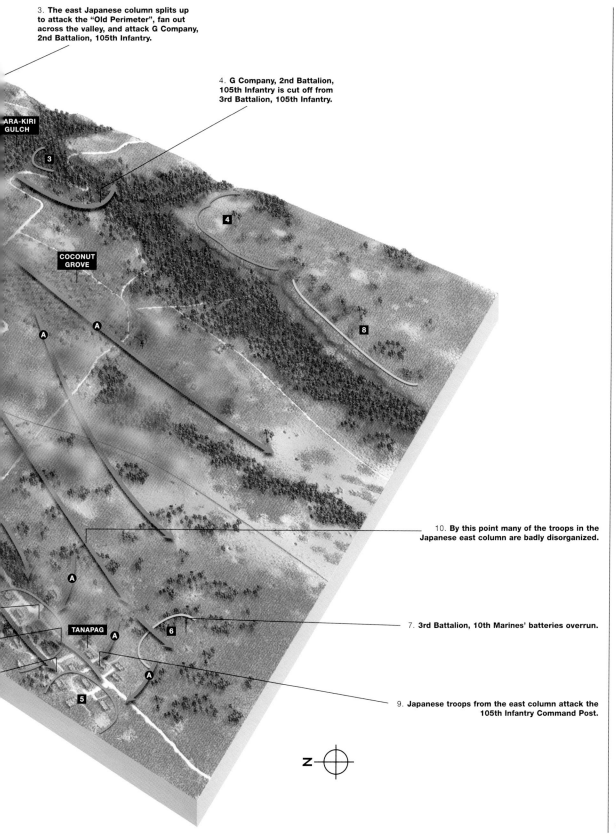

3. **The east Japanese column splits up to attack the "Old Perimeter", fan out across the valley, and attack G Company, 2nd Battalion, 105th Infantry.**

4. **G Company, 2nd Battalion, 105th Infantry is cut off from 3rd Battalion, 105th Infantry.**

ARA-KIRI GULCH

3

4

COCONUT GROVE

8

A

A

A

10. **By this point many of the troops in the Japanese east column are badly disorganized.**

A

7. **3rd Battalion, 10th Marines' batteries overrun.**

TANAPAG A

6

A

9. **Japanese troops from the east column attack the 105th Infantry Command Post.**

5

Z

CAPTURE AND OCCUPATION OF TINIAN

From the very beginning, the necessity of seizing Tinian, 3 miles (4.8km) south of Saipan, was understood. There would be a constant threat of raids and artillery attacks from the 9,000-man Japanese garrison if not eliminated. The island was also needed as the location for additional airbases. Saipan and Guam alone were insufficient to accommodate the projected Twentieth Air Force units and their massive support infrastructure, along with Army and Marine staging bases. Advanced planning and preparations for the assault of Tinian began while the vicious battle for Saipan continued.

Preliminaries and Selecting the Beaches

Just over a week after 15 June Saipan landing, Army 155mm Long Tom guns began shelling Tinian from the south end of the larger island. Soon, 13 Army and Marine battalions of XXIV Corps Artillery were concentrated on Saipan's south end to interdict targets on Tinian and support the upcoming assault. This included eight 105mm and three 155mm howitzer, and two 155mm gun battalions – 168 tubes. The 27th InfDiv retained only its 106th Field Artillery Battalion. Naval bombardment of Tinian occurred frequently while fighting continued on Saipan, and bombardments increased after 26 June.

J-Day was set for 24 July. The Guam assault would begin on the 21st. On 10 July the 4th and 2nd MarDivs began preparations for Tinian. The 4th MarDiv would lead the assault with the 2nd coming ashore on J+1. The exhausted 4th accepted the mission with grim resignation. It would be its third assault landing in less than six months. Both divisions had suffered heavy losses during 24 days of intense combat, a combined total of 1,363 dead and missing and 10,419 wounded. There were also

Pontoon causeways were emplaced on both "White 1" and "White 2" reaching to the reef's edge to allow vehicles to roll ashore directly from landing craft without wading and speeding up the landing of equipment and supplies. This "White 2" causeway was damaged by artillery fire on the afternoon of 27 July (J+3). Both causeways were destroyed by a storm on the night of 29/30 July.

An M4A2 Sherman tank of the 4th Tank Battalion crosses the rising ground on the north slopes of Mt. Lasso. It is followed by a 75mm gun-armed M3 halftrack. In the background are the flat cane fields extending to the "White" beaches.

significant numbers of combat fatigue cases, illness, and non-combat injuries. A couple of thousand wounded had been returned to duty and more were returned to their units as the battle for Tinian was fought. On 11 July the 2nd MarDiv received an inadequate 848 replacements and the 4th 845. Regardless, the battalions averaged 565 men rather than the Table of Organization 954. The divisions were able to rest and reorganize while the 27th InfDiv mopped up on Saipan. 1/29 Marines was attached to the Saipan Garrison Force.

The 4th MarDiv was heavily augmented with an unprecedented three Marine and three Army amphibian tractor battalions, a Marine armored amphibian tractor battalion, and an Army amphibian tank battalion along with the 2nd MarDiv's tank battalion, two 75mm howitzer battalions, and two DUKW companies. 543 amtracs, 68 amphibian tanks, and 140 DUKWs would be used.

Most of Tinian was edged with jagged limestone cliffs between 6 and 100ft (1.8–31m) high, presenting a difficulty for invasion planners. While the island was fringed with coral reefs, these did not pose the problems the cliffs did. Gaps in the cliffs were few and narrow allowing the defenders to concentrate on the most likely landing sites.

The best beaches were located on the southwest shore at Tinian Town on Sunharon Bay. This is also where the Japanese expected the Americans to land and contained the highest concentration of troops, including numerous 25mm twin AA guns and extensive infantry defenses. It was also covered by two coast defense batteries and was heavily mined. The four beaches, designated "Orange", "Red", "Green", and "Blue", were 2,100yds (1,920m) wide in total, but were separated by sections of low cliffs between 200 and 2,000yds (183–1,829m) wide.

Another possible site was Beach "Yellow" on the northeast shore at Asiga Bay. While considered the second most likely beach by the Japanese commander, it consisted of gaps in the 20–25ft-high (6.1–7.6m) cliffs only 125yds (114m) wide. The bay was covered by 23 pillboxes and two coast defense batteries.

Two other beaches existed, "White 1" and "White 2", on the northwest shore. Colonel Ogata considered "White 2" to be a possible secondary landing site and directed light defenses to be established there. Regardless,

On Tinian's flat cane fields a line of skirmishers was the preferred formation as the Marines searched for scattered Japanese emplacements. In the background is the ridgeline stretching south from Mt. Lasso, which is off to the right of the photograph. This places the area on the island's east side in the 2nd MarDiv zone.

the Japanese did not consider the "White" beaches as viable options; they were simply too small. "White 1" was located 1,000yds (914m) west of the end of Airfield No. 1. It was only 60yds (55m) wide, hardly the usual 1,200yds (1,097m) desired for a regiment landing with two battalions abreast. "White 2" was 1,000yds (914m) to the southwest of "White 1". It was 160yds (146m) wide, but only the center 65yds (59m) was free of coral outcroppings and ledges.

Because of the extent of defenses on the other beaches, the fact that the assault troops would be weary after a prolonged and difficult fight on Saipan, and that Tinian could be secured at a comparatively leisurely pace, American planners were led to seriously consider the "White" beaches, regardless of their drawbacks.

On the night of 10/11 July, recon marines of Amphibious Reconnaissance Battalion, VAC and frogmen from UDT-5 and 7 were dropped from destroyers, paddled inshore in rubber boats, and then swam in to investigate the "White" and "Yellow" beaches. As expected the "Yellow" Beach defenses were strong and being strengthened further. The recon marines and frogmen targeting "White 2" were swept northeast by a strong current, but landed on "White 1" and successfully reconnoitered it. This was fortunate as the "White 1" team was also swept away, but successfully reconnoitered "White 2" the next night.

The "White" beach reports confirmed the aerial reconnaissance assessment and the lack of man-made obstacles or mines. Other than small potholes and boulders, the coral reefs were free of natural obstacles. The reports were presented to Adm Turner, who remained dubious. Turner's boss, Vice Adm Spruance, agreed with the "White" plan, but was reluctant to order Turner to accept the plan and called a meeting aboard his flagship. Turner's staff presented the plan favorably and all of Hill's Navy and Marine commanders agreed. Spruance asked Turner for his opinion and he agreed to accept the plan if the reconnaissance reports were favorable. Turner's operation plan was issued the next day. H-Hour, J-Day (Jig-Day), was set at 07.30hrs, 24 July.

The tiny "White" beaches precluded the usual practice of landing and stockpiling supplies on the beaches and then moving them forward to frontline units. Supplies would have to be hauled inland by LVTs and

DUKWs and dumps established well clear of the beaches. The lead assault regiments would, therefore, in addition to closing with and destroying the enemy, have to link up, establishing a single beachhead, and plunge inland as far and as fast as resistance permitted to provide the depth necessary for supply dumps, artillery positions, command posts, aid stations, and reserve units.

On 12 July MajGen Schmidt assumed command of VAC/NTLF to allow LtGen Smith to oversee the Guam operation and MajGen Cates took command of the 4th MarDiv. The Army Garrison Force assumed control of Saipan.

Embarkation for the short trip to Tinian began on 20 July with loading conducted at Tanapag Harbor and the "Red", "Blue", and "Yellow" beaches. Ten assault and troop transports, two LSDs, 37 LSTs, 31 LCIs, 20 LCTs, 92 LCMs, 100 LCVPs, and 14 pontoon barges supported the operation. The 2nd and 8th Marines of the 2nd MarDiv were loaded aboard seven of the transports to conduct the J-Day demonstration. The 6th Marines would be picked up by LSTs after off-loading amtracs at Tinian. Much effort was made to streamline logistics, for example, the NTLF and 4th MarDiv's Shore Parties were combined and would also support the 2nd MarDiv. On 21 July (W-Day) the 3rd MarDiv and 1st Prov MarBde landed on Guam. The Tinian landing force departed Saipan on the night of the 23rd.

On 16 July, the naval bombardment of Tinian was again increased and surprise bombardments delivered day and night on Japanese troops constructing defenses. The day before the assault three battleships, five cruisers, and 16 destroyers delivered concentrated bombardments on all obvious beaches, but only cursory shelling took place of targets in the vicinity of the "White" beaches for deception purposes. However, the USS *Colorado* (BB-45) knocked out the three 140mm guns on Faibus San Hilo Point that covered the "White" beaches. Air attacks began in earnest on 22 June. Destroyers fired white phosphorus rounds into the cane fields to burn them off, but the fields were wet and these efforts were of only limited success. A total of 358 aircraft struck Tinian on J-1, dropping

A Marine reserve unit following the skirmish line passes a dugout of the type the skirmishers were in search of. The shredded sandbags and blasted away vegetation attest to the firepower directed at the position.

97 tons of bombs plus 200 rockets. During the pre-landing bombardment, three previously unknown and well-concealed 150mm guns opened fire on the USS *Colorado*, scoring 22 hits, and the USS *Norman Scott* (DD-690), achieving six hits. The *Colorado* suffered 43 dead (including 10 Marines) and 198 wounded (32 Marines) while the *Norman Scott* lost 19 dead and 47 wounded.

J-Day

24 June began with a temperature of 70°F (21.1°C), visibility of 5–7 miles (8–11km) with smoke and dust from the bombardment, moderate south winds, the sea was lightly choppy, with no surf on the "White" beaches but a strong northeast running tidal current.

From 05.57 to 10.15hrs, the 2nd MarDiv conducted a feint off Tinian Town to reinforce the enemy's belief that the main assault would take place here. After the demonstration force withdrew, the Japanese command signaled Tokyo that an attack had been repulsed. The feint, however, succeeded in holding the defenders in place rather than allowing them to deploy north. Air attacks swept the island between lulls in the gunfire of the bombardment force and XXIV Corps Artillery on southern Saipan. The LVTs disembarked from their LSTs at 06.00 and began circling as assault waves assembled. A rainstorm foiled UDT frogmen attempting to destroy coral boulders and anti-boat mines on "White 2". A battleship, two cruisers, and four destroyers supporting the assault fired directly into the beaches in the hope of destroying mines. Thirty LCI gunboats fired 40mm and 20mm guns, and 4.5in. rockets into the beach areas. This was followed by on-call aircraft strikes. Air observers reported possible mines remaining on the beaches. The assault waves were a little slow in assembling and H-Hour was moved to 07.40hrs. Long Tom guns on Saipan laid smoke on Mt. Lasso to deny the Japanese observation of the beaches. The Marine amtracs churned shoreward regardless of possible mines. Further delay would allow the Japanese to reinforce the "White" beaches, a more deadly prospect than the mines.

On "White 1" E/2/24 Marines came ashore in LVTs at 07.47hrs to discover that the few anti-boat mines there had been allowed to deteriorate. A small defense detachment gave Marines climbing the low cliffs from waist-deep water a bad time, but immediate resistance was light. The rest of the battalion followed in a column of companies, as did 1/24. Eliminating resistance from caves and crevasses, the 24th Marines had secured its O-1 Line 1,400yds (1,280m) inland, by 16.00hrs.

The 25th Marines assaulting "White 2" took advantage of the wider beach and landed two battalions abreast, with both battalions in company column. I/3/25 landed on the left in 16 LVTs and G/2/25 on the right. The 2nd Battalion's other two companies managed to land abreast for greater speed in crossing the beach. Under scattered smallarms fire some LVTs nosed up to the cliff in the choppy water to allow marines to climb over them. Resistance stiffened as the 25th Marines pushed inland. The dozen or so anti-boat mines surviving on this beach were still functional. The Marines avoided the main beach until engineers cleared the mines by 13.37hrs. More mines were found inland after two amtracs hit them. A mine on the beach destroyed another. Booby traps were found in the area and a more substantial defense force was present. Japanese mortars, AT guns, and artillery pounded the area. Caves, ravines, and field fortifications were positioned in-depth. The stiff resistance prevented the 25th Marines from reaching its O-1 Line and Mt. Maga. However, the regiments quickly established contact between the two beaches.

A single LVT-delivered ramp was emplaced below "White 1" to allow amtracs to push inland and drop off supplies; a second ramped LVT had overturned. M4A2 medium, M5A1 light, and M3A1 flame-tanks landed on "White 2" and were instrumental in reducing resistance in both beach areas. Six more LVT ramps were emplaced on J+1 and assisted the landing of the 2nd Tank Battalion.

The 4th MarDiv commander was more concerned about being prepared to withstand the expected counterattack than reaching the O-1 Line. He ordered the advance to halt at 16.30hrs. The regimental reserve battalions had landed by early afternoon and the Division

Called "The Cliff" by the Marines, the 500–580ft (152–177m) ridge on the south end of Tinian proved to be tough to clear. Most of the remaining Japanese had withdrawn there and they launched numerous attacks and harassing actions on the Marines as they fought their way up and over the ridge. Densely covered by brush, the ridge provided countless hiding places for the remnants in caves and ravines.

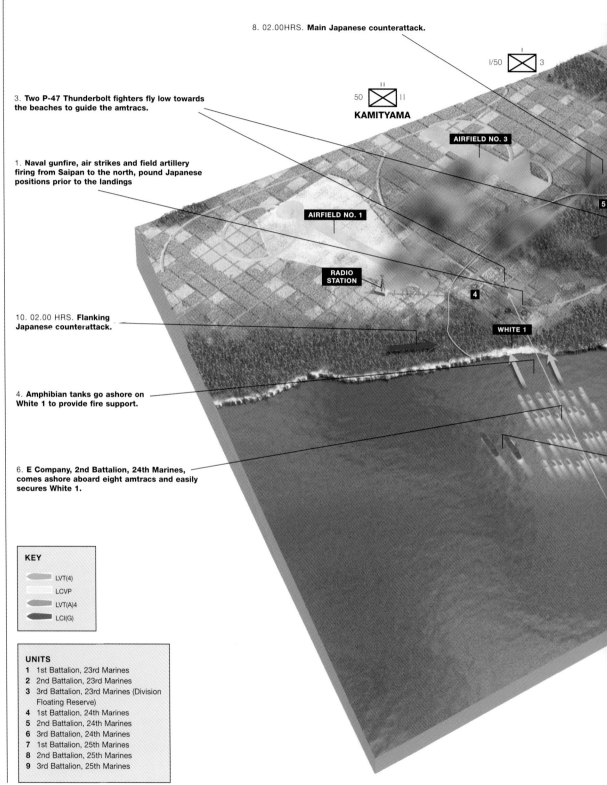

8. 02.00HRS. **Main Japanese counterattack.**

I/50 ⊠ 3

50 ⊠ II
KAMITYAMA

3. **Two P-47 Thunderbolt fighters fly low towards the beaches to guide the amtracs.**

AIRFIELD NO. 3

1. **Naval gunfire, air strikes and field artillery firing from Saipan to the north, pound Japanese positions prior to the landings**

5

AIRFIELD NO. 1

RADIO STATION

4

10. 02.00 HRS. **Flanking Japanese counterattack.**

WHITE 1

4. **Amphibian tanks go ashore on White 1 to provide fire support.**

6. **E Company, 2nd Battalion, 24th Marines, comes ashore aboard eight amtracs and easily secures White 1.**

KEY

LVT(4)
LCVP
LVT(A)4
LCI(G)

UNITS
1 1st Battalion, 23rd Marines
2 2nd Battalion, 23rd Marines
3 3rd Battalion, 23rd Marines (Division
    Floating Reserve)
4 1st Battalion, 24th Marines
5 2nd Battalion, 24th Marines
6 3rd Battalion, 24th Marines
7 1st Battalion, 25th Marines
8 2nd Battalion, 25th Marines
9 3rd Battalion, 25th Marines

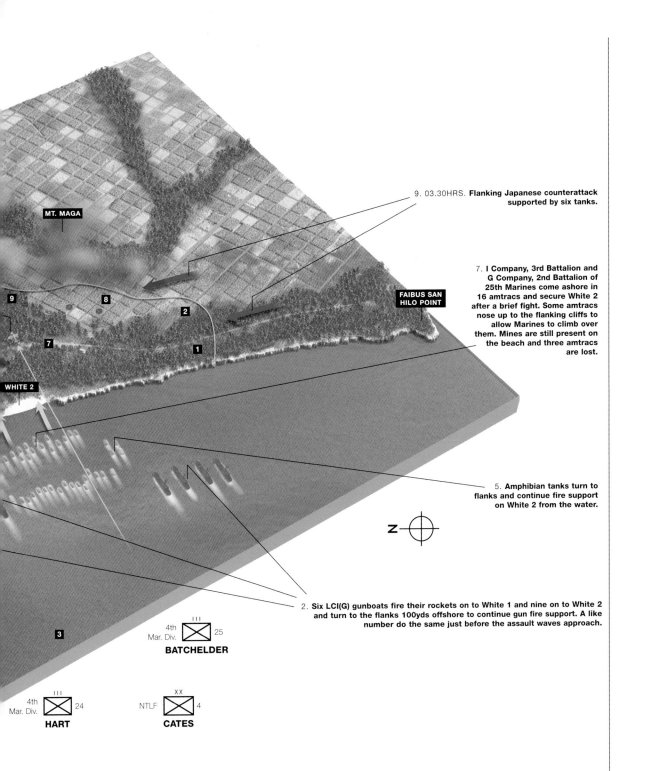

9. 03.30HRS. **Flanking Japanese counterattack supported by six tanks.**

7. **I Company, 3rd Battalion and G Company, 2nd Battalion of 25th Marines come ashore in 16 amtracs and secure White 2 after a brief fight. Some amtracs nose up to the flanking cliffs to allow Marines to climb over them. Mines are still present on the beach and three amtracs are lost.**

5. **Amphibian tanks turn to flanks and continue fire support on White 2 from the water.**

2. **Six LCI(G) gunboats fire their rockets on to White 1 and nine on to White 2 and turn to the flanks 100yds offshore to continue gun fire support. A like number do the same just before the assault waves approach.**

MT. MAGA

FAIBUS SAN HILO POINT

WHITE 2

9 | 8 | 2 | 7 | 1 | 3

Z

4th Mar. Div. ⊠ 25
BATCHELDER

4th Mar. Div. ⊠ 24
HART

NTLF ⊠ 4
CATES

J-DAY, TINIAN

24 July 1944, viewed from the northwest showing the 24th and 25th Marines' assault on beaches "White 1" and "White 2" and the subsequent Japanese counterattacks against the marines' night perimeter.

Reserve, the 23rd Marines, was ordered to land that morning, but severe communications problems delayed this until 14.00hrs. In the event this proved fortunate, as the degree of congestion would not have allowed room for another regiment to land. The Regiment landed on "White 2" and went into the line to the right of the 25th Marines. 3/23 was designated the Division Reserve. Barbed wire was strung across the 7,000yd (6,400m) beachhead and 75mm halftrack-mounted guns, 37mm AT guns, and bazookas positioned on avenues of approach suitable for tanks. The first day on Tinian resulted in 15 Marines KIA and 225 WIA, but 438 enemy dead were counted. Despite the small beaches, mines, resistance, and rain, 15,614 Marines were ashore.

Japanese probes began at 22.30hrs and counterattacks began at midnight to last all night in the form of screaming *banzai* charges. IJN troops attacked the 24th Marines on the northeast side of the beachhead at 02.00hrs. IJA troops attacked the 23rd Marines anchored on the shore on the southwest side of the beachhead at 03.30. A series of counterattacks was launched at the beachhead's center on the boundary between the 25th and 24th Marines. A company-size force managed to reach the beach area, but was wiped out. The Marines suffered fewer than 100 casualties. The Japanese lost over 1,200 dead and five tanks.

The Drive South (J+1 to J+6)

The primary goal on 25 July was to expand the beachhead and land the 2nd MarDiv. The 8th Marines came ashore on "White 1" by noon, immediately followed by the 2nd Marines. The 8th was initially attached to the 4th MarDiv on the left flank and surged toward Ushi Point. The 2nd MarDiv command group came ashore on "White 1" and most of the 6th Marines were ashore by late afternoon having been picked up on Saipan by LSTs in the late morning. 2/6 was the Division Reserve and the 4th MarDiv (less 8th Marines) was the NTLF Reserve. The planned 07.00hrs 4th MarDiv attack was delayed until 11.00 because of the need to reorganize and resupply after the all-night fight for the beachhead. The beachhead was expanded beyond the O-1 Line with the 25th Marines taking Mt. Maga by double envelopment. The 23rd Marines pushed out on the right flank slightly beyond Mt. Maga. The 8th Marines, clearing the broad Ushi Point area, had left a gap between itself and the 24th Marines, forcing it to place its reserve battalion in the line. The 14th Marines' four 75mm pack howitzer battalions, including two from the 2nd MarDiv, suffered from counter-battery fire. Most of the casualties the regiment suffered were lost on this day. The night saw only minor infiltration attempts and no repeat of the wasteful *banzai* changes.

The 2nd MarDiv took over the eastern portion of the line on the morning of J+2 (26 July) and easily cleared the northeast end of the island south to Asiga Point overlooking Asiga Bay. All 2nd MarDiv units attached to the 4th MarDiv were ordered released back to the parent division at 06.30hrs. The 6th Marines completed their landing. In the west, the 4th MarDiv had to contend with securing Mt. Lasso, however. 1/25 Marines seized the mountain at 16.30hrs, experiencing only light resistance. Despite the small beaches the flow of supplies ashore continued unabated, in spite of the "White 2" pontoon causeway being damaged by artillery fire. Also on 26 July, the 4th MarDiv's 3/14 Marines arrived from Saipan, being the first 105mm battalion to come ashore.

The south end of Tinian was honeycombed with caves in which hundreds of Japanese troops and civilians hid. The water's edge was the O-8 Line, the final objective. Even though the island was declared secure on 1 August (J+8), it would be a week before these cliffs were cleared by the 8th Marines.

Enemy contact was extremely light on J+3 and +4. The gently rolling cane fields provided little defendable terrain. The Marines would advance with riflemen in line and skirmishers forward, tanks interspaced across a battalion's front. On 27 July the advance in the 4th MarDiv's zone was slow as gains were consolidated on the high ground, but nevertheless reached the O-4 Line. The 4th 105mm Howitzer Battalion was attached to the Division on 27 July. The 2nd MarDiv made more headway on easier terrain and went beyond the O-4 Line. The Division's 3/10 and 4/10 Marines arrived with their 105mm howitzers.

On 28 July the situation reversed itself with the 4th MarDiv making the greater advance, going well beyond the O-5 Line. Also on 28 July, the Ushi Point Airfield was able to receive fighter aircraft. Although casualties had been light, the units were under strength and the 2nd MarDiv received 862 replacements while the 4th MarDiv received 850. The Marines had experienced rain and gusty wind from J-Day, but on 28 July the weather turned foul with high winds and rainstorms. The causeways were damaged by high seas and unloading operations were suspended. As on Saipan there were shortages of mortar ammunition, particularly 81mm light high explosive and 60mm illumination. 75mm ammunition was also short as was fuel and oil, forcing Marines to use captured aviation gasoline in their vehicles.

On 29 July (J+5) both divisions pressed forward with over half the island now secured. Despite the hiatus in resupply, adequate supplies were on hand and enemy resistance light and the regiments were urged forward. From west to east the line included the 24th, 25th, 6th, and 2nd Marines. Both divisions again made good headway on J+6 (30 July) with the 4th MarDiv securing Tinian Town and Airfield No. 4 against light resistance while 2nd MarDiv cleared the 340–380 Ridge on the lower east coast. Moderate resistance was experienced on the south portion of the ridge, but was never well organized. Also on 30 July, 2/2 Marines were designated the NTLF Reserve.

LVT(2)S EMPLACE CLIFF RAMPS, BEACH "WHITE 1", TINIAN
(pages 82–83)

A novel idea was proposed by Navy Capt Paul J. Halloran, a Seabee and the NTLF construction officer, in an effort to widen Tinian's small beaches. Capt Halloran drew up plans for an unusual modification of the obsolescent LVT(2) amtrac (1). He reasoned that the 6–10ft limestone cliffs flanking the "White" beaches could be surmounted by ramps to allow LVTs to clamber inland and reduce traffic congestion on the narrow beaches. They could not be constructed on-site as time was of the essence. Undoubtedly, the beach area would be under fire, making it suicidal for on-site ramp construction crews. The ramps had to be emplaced as early as possible to allow the rapid expansion of the beachhead. Capt Halloran's plans called for two 25ft-long 10in.-high, 6in.-wide steel I-beams (2) to be attached to the sides of an LVT(2) and angled upward from the bow at 45 degrees. The girders were attached to three 6ft-long vertical 6 x 12in. timbers bolted to the side sponsons (3). An articulated ramp of 18 13ft-long, 6 x 12in. timbers was constructed by boring three holes from edge to edge and running steel cables through them (4). The two outer cables were sheathed by 2in.-diameter

6in.-long sections of pipe to maintain spacing between timbers. The first six timbers of the ramp rested on the forward portion of the elevated I-beams. Only the first timber was actually bolted to the beams. The rest laid like a mat atop horizontal angle-iron bars bolted to the LVT's deck (5). The idea was for the LVT to approach the cliff, nose the top end of the ramp and I-beams on to the cliff top and back off a few feet. Seabees (6) jumped over either side and released the retaining chains holding the I-beams to the vertical side timbers. The lower (back) ends of the I-beams dropped on to the beach and the amtrac continued to back off. The rest of the ramp slid off the top of the LVT to rest on the inclined I-beams. A ramp capable of supporting LVTs, halftracks, and even 32.5-ton M4A2 tanks had been emplaced in a matter of minutes. Ten LVT(2)s were so modified by the 2nd Amphibian Tractor Battalion and transported to Tinian aboard the USS *Ashland* (LSD-1) (7). Seabee battalions established ramp maintenance units to maintain, that is, replace the ramp's timbers. LVTs and tanks quickly chewed them up. While small in number, the seven LVT ramps actually emplaced served to open much-needed additional beach exit points on "White 1". (Howard Gerrard)

As on Saipan, many Japanese civilians and troops threw themselves from the cliffs between Lalo and Marpo Points. Loudspeaker-equipped jeeps were used by Japanese-American interpreters in often futile efforts to convince them that they would not be harmed if they gave themselves up.

The Last Fight (J+7 to J+8)

An unnamed ridge, ranging from 500 to 580ft (152m–177m) in height, dominated Tinian's south end between Lalo and Marpo Points. It had steep cliffs all round and was honeycombed with caves, ravines, and coral outcroppings. The ridge top was a relatively open plateau. Hundreds of Japanese troops, the remnants of numerous units, were now cornered on this rugged promontory. From west to east the 24th, 23rd, 8th, 6th, and 2nd Marines faced the brush-covered cliffs and were set to attack at 08.30hrs, 31 July. Two battleships, three cruisers, and 13 destroyers fired a massive preparatory barrage, along with divisional and corps artillery and both fighter and bomber strikes. The struggle up the cliffs and the reduction of the ridge was a tough fight with enemy defenses being dense and in-depth in well-concealed positions. On the west flank the 24th Marines made the most headway on the less steep portion of the cliff and also secured the road to the ridge top. The 2nd Marines on the east flank had the primary mission of sealing off the base of the ridge and preventing the enemy from fleeing up the east coast. Facing the steepest section of the cliff, the 6th Marines stalled, but the 8th was able to establish a toehold on the zigzag road to the top. It was possible to deploy armor, and tank guns, flame-tanks, and self-propelled guns helped reduce the caves. The first night on the ridge was brutal: a 600yd (549m) gap had developed between the divisions and several smaller gaps existed because of the chaotic terrain. Japanese probes and counterattacks began at 01.00hrs. A 150-man force managed to block the road in the 8th Marines' rear area and destroyed a number of vehicles. At 05.15hrs a *banzai* charge was launched in the 2/8 Marines zone by up to 700 Japanese.

The morning of 1 August (J+8) found the Marines still holding their positions of the previous night. With a toehold on the plateau the 4th MarDiv launched its attack at 08.00hrs. The 23rd Marines were halted by a sheer cliff and had to retrace their steps back down the ridge, rejoining the line alongside the 24th Marines at the base of the cliff on the coastal low ground near Lalo Point. The 2nd MarDiv would have to fight down the terraced ridge toward the rugged coast and the O-8 Line. The 6th and 8th Marines cleared the cave-riddled cliffs while the 2nd Marines continued to prevent any Japanese from escaping up the east coast. Resistance was light in most areas and large numbers of civilians began to

Ushi Point

25 Jul
0–2
0–1

III 8

White 1
III 8

White 2
Airfield 1

III 2
Airfield 3

0–3

24 Jul
0–1
25 Jul

III 24

III 25
III 23
Mt Maga

0–4A
III 6
III 2

Asiga Point
26 Jul

Faibus San Hilo Point
0–2/FBHL
III 23

III 25 Mt Lasso

FBHL

0–3
0–4

26 Jul
0–4A

Yellow

27 Jul
III 23

Asiga Bay

III 24

III 25

0–4
0–5
0–6

0–5
XX 2
27 Jul

XX 4
4 2
XX

28 Jul
III 2

Masalog Point

29 Jul

Airfield 2

0–7A

28 Jul
III 24

III 25
III 6

Gurguan Point

0–6A
0–6

0–7

29 Jul
0–7
30 Jul

Orange

Airfield 4
III 2

Tinian Town
III 6

Red 1
Red 2
III 8

Green 1
Green 2
0–7

30 Jul
III 23

0–8A
31 Jul

Sunharon Harbor
Blue
III 24
III 6

III 8

Marpo Point
0–8

1 Aug

31 Jul

0–8

N

Unit boundary line
Progress line
O–Line/FBHL
O–A–Line

The island is covered with sugar cane
apart from scrub or bush covered slopes

0   2 miles
0   2 km

Lalo Point

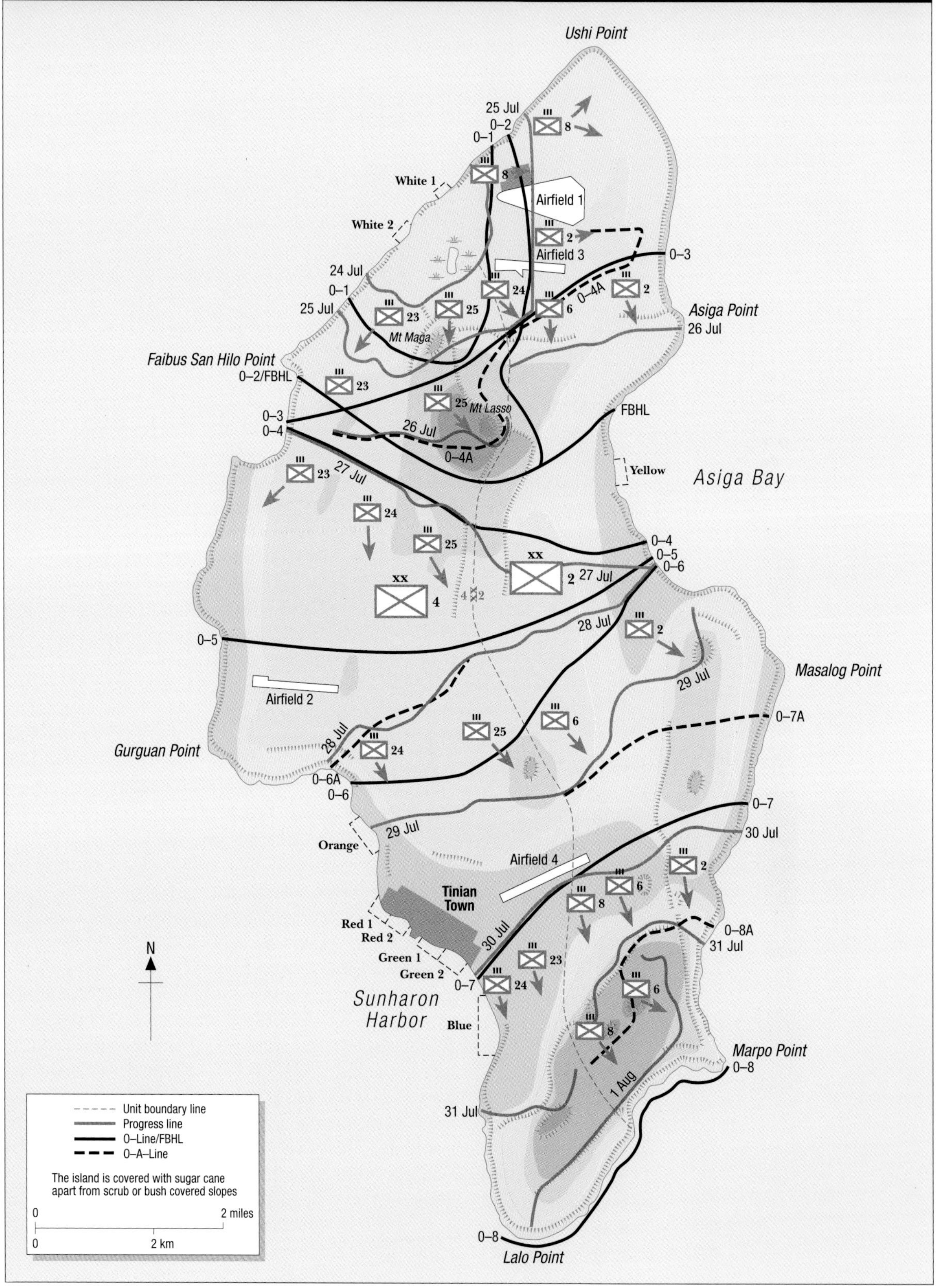

emerge and turn themselves in. Even though the 6th Marines had not yet reached Marpo Point, MajGen Schmidt declared Tinian secure at 18.55hrs.

Significant numbers of Japanese still held out in the coastal cliffs and there is some controversy over whether the island was declared secure too soon. Between 100–250 Japanese attacked the 3/6 Marines CP with most killed and the Marines suffering only light casualties. Smaller last-ditch attacks occurred through 3 August. Though disorganized, resistance was still encountered. More civilians surrendered and although others committed suicide, the mass suicides witnessed on Saipan were not repeated. However, large numbers of civilians were murdered by Japanese troops by tying them up in groups of 15–20 and blowing them up with demolitions or throwing them over cliffs. Mopping-up continued with so many caves being found that there were not enough demolitions to seal them. On 4 August the 4th MarDiv turned over the sector it was mopping-up to the 23rd Marines while the 8th Marines took over responsibility for the 2nd MarDiv sector. On 7 August the 8th Marines relieved the 23rd Marines as well. Almost 400 Japanese were killed in the week after the island was secured.

The 2nd MarDiv was moved back to Saipan in August to continue mopping-up there. The 8th Marines was attached to Island Command, Tinian on 10 August. The Regiment, less its 1st Battalion, relocated to Saipan on 25 October. 1/8 remained until 1 January 1945. The 2nd MarDiv would later act as the IIIAC Floating Reserve at Okinawa and the 8th Marines would fight ashore. The 4th MarDiv sailed back to Maui, Hawaii, in mid-August to rebuild and in February 1945 it assaulted Iwo Jima. VAC also returned to Hawaii and there the former Expeditionary Troops Staff (VAC Blue Staff) became Headquarters, FMFPac while the NTLF Staff (VAC Red Staff) became the new VAC Staff.

AFTERMATH

The battle for Saipan was a decisive engagement, both militarily and politically. Japan's National Defense Zone was pierced, the Japanese Navy suffered a critical defeat from which it could not recover, and an American base was secured from which B-29 bombers could attack the Home Islands. Although one of the Mandated islands, Saipan was considered practically Japanese territory because of its heavy colonization. The impact of the Saipan landing in Japan was serious. On 26 June, well before Saipan fell, Emperor Hirohito requested that the Foreign Minister find a diplomatic way to end the war. The Japanese Government delayed announcing the island's fall and when it did Prime Minster, War Minister, and Chief of Army General Staff Tojo Hideki and his cabinet were forced to resign on 18 July. The Navy Minister and the Chief of the Navy General Staff also stepped down.

The assault and occupation of Saipan and Tinian was costly, with a total of 18,471 Marine and Army casualties. Further casualties were suffered over the following months during Garrison Force mopping-up. A total of 505 sailors were lost aboard ships struck by coast defense guns, on landing craft, and ashore.

Saipan US Casualties

Unit	Strength	KIA/MIA	WIA	Total
NTLF/VAC Troops	3,062	22	130	152
XXIV Corps Artillery	3,631	7	18	25
2d MarDiv (+)	21,746	1,256	4,914	6,170
4th MarDiv (+)	21,618	1,107	5,505	6,612
27th InfDiv (+)	16,404	1,034	2,532	3,566
Total	67,451	3,426	13,099	16,525

Six Army KIA and 16 WIA during the 10 July–6 August 1944 mopping-up.

Tinian US Casualties

Unit	KIA	WIA	Total
NTLF/VAC Troops	2	8	10
XXIV Corps Artillery	—	3	3
2d MarDiv (+)	105	653	758
4th MarDiv (+)	212	897	1,109
Prov Amtrac Group, VAC	7	32	39 [8]
Total	326 [9]	1,593	1,946

38 Marines were KIA and 125 WIA during the 2 August 1944–1 January 1945 mopping-up.

Of the 31,629 Japanese troops on Saipan, 23,811 were given burials with many more sealed up in bunkers and caves. An estimated 29,500 Japanese troops died. A total of 952 Japanese and 838 Koreans were captured. Almost 300 more surrendered after the fighting and the 27th InfDiv killed another 1,972 during mopping-up by the end of September. An estimated

22,000 Japanese, Okinawan, and Korean civilians committed suicide, were murdered by Japanese troops to prevent their surrender, or were killed by Japanese or American fire. Many native civilians suffered the same fate. In September 1945 the number of interned civilians included 13,954 Japanese, 1,411 Koreans, 2,966 Chamorros, and 1,025 Carolinians.

Of the 8,039 Japanese on Tinian over 5,000 dead were counted with thousands more buried in caves and bunkers. Island Command killed another 542 after the island was secured. Only 252 prisoners were taken. By 10 August, 13,000 Japanese civilians had been interned. As on Saipan up to 4,000 had committed suicide, were murdered by Japanese troops, or were killed in combat action.

The Japanese lost thousands of sailors during the battle of the Philippine Sea. Thousands more sailors and troops were lost aboard transports and other ships sunk in the vicinity of the Marianas before and during the battle.

The Army Air Forces began building two massive airfields for B-29 bombers, Kobler and Isely Fields. Aslito Airfield was first renamed Conroy Field on 18 June. XXI Bomber Command renamed it Isley Field, the name most commonly used; it was named after Commander Robert H. Isely, a Navy pilot killed during the battle for Saipan. Today it is known as Iseley International Airport. Isely was fully operational by mid-December 1944 and was the main operating field, with Kobler being used for spare bombers and transport flights. The former Japanese railroad was restored and operational before the fighting was over. By 25 July Tanapag Harbor had been cleared allowing its use, and on 1 September Navy Operating Base, Saipan was commissioned. The seaplane base at Flores Point was rebuilt and naval depots, repair bases, and support facilities constructed. The Navy competed the 4,500ft (1,372m) former Japanese airfield at Marpi Point in July 1945 extending it to 7,000ft (2,134m) and building a second 3,500ft (1,067m) runway. A new 5,000ft (1,524m) airfield was built on Kagman Peninsula.

Naval Base, Tinian was established at Tinian Town as a cargo ship port to supply bomber units. The island was literally leveled when new airfields were constructed; over 8,000,000 cubic yards of coral fill were used to construct the six main runways, taxiways, and hardstands. Immense support facilities were built. The first was the 6,000ft (1,829m) West Field built for the Navy in November 1944 over the old Airfield No. 2. Two 8,500ft (2,591m) runways were added to West Field and it was taken over by the Army Air Forces for B-29 operations. It was ready in March 1945, though still used by the Navy as Naval Air Base, Tinian. North Field was built over the old No. 1 and 3 Airfields. It was operational in February 1945 and by May had four 8,500ft (2,591m) B-29 runways. An aerial mine depot was built to support B-29s mining Japanese ports and assembled more mines than all other US mine depots together. It was from Tinian that B-29s launched to drop atomic bombs on Hiroshima and Nagasaki on 6 and 9 August 1945.

---

8 Includes Marine and Army.
9 KIA total does not include 27 MIA in both divisions, which have been added to the total casualties.

ORDERS OF BATTLE: US AND JAPANESE FORCES, SAIPAN & TINIAN

US UNIT ORGANIZATION TABLES

Northern Attack Force (TF 52)
1 heavy cruiser   Vice Adm R.K. Turner (to 15 Jul)
Second-in-Command (TG 52.2)   Rear Adm W.H. Hill
1 amphibious command ship [10]
Transport Group "Able" (TG 52.3)   Capt H.B. Knowles
Transport Group "Baker" (TG 52.4)   Capt D.W. Loomis
Eastern Landing Group (TG 52.8)   Comdr C.J. McWhinnie
Transport Screen (TG 52.12)   Capt R.E. Libby
Tractor Flotilla (TG 52.5)   Capt A.J. Robertson
Control Group (TG 52.6)   Comdr P.S. Theiss
Fire Support Group 1 (TG 52.17)   Rear Adm J.B. Oldendorf
Fire Support Group 2 (TG 52.10)   Rear Adm W.L. Ainsworth
Carrier Support Group 1 (TG 52.14)   Rear Adm G.F. Bogan
Carrier Support Group 2 (TG 52.11)   Rear Adm H.B. Sallada
Minesweeping & Hydrographic Survey Group (TG 52.13)   Cdr R.S. Moore
Service & Salvage Group (TG 52.7)   Capt S.E. Peck
Joint Expeditionary Force Reserve (TG 51.1)   Rear Adm W.H.P. Blandy

SAIPAN

Northern Troops and Landing Force (TG 56.1)/VAC
VAC HQ&S Battalion (-)
VAC Amphibious Reconnaissance Battalion (- Company A)
VAC Medical Battalion (-)
VAC Signal Battalion (-)
VAC MT Company (-)
VAC Shore Party (NTLF Shore Party)
VAC Prov LVT Group (-)
VAC Prov Engineer Group (-)
2nd Separate Engineer Battalion
7th Field Depot (+) (-)
    3rd Marine Ammunition Company
    18th, 19th, and 20th Marine Depot Companies
31st Medical Field Hospital (US Army)
2nd and 3rd Prov Portable Surgical Hospitals (US Army)
Air Warning Squadron (Air Transportable) 5 (-) [11]
Detachments, 680th, 726th, and 763rd Aircraft Warning Signal Companies (USAAF)
Detachment, Company C, 101st Signal Battalion, Separate (US Army)

XXIV Corps Artillery (US Army)
    420th Field Artillery Group (US Army)
        2nd Battalion, 55th Coast Artillery Regiment (155mm Gun) (Mobile)
        32nd Coast Artillery Gun Battalion (155mm Gun)
        145th Field Artillery Battalion (155mm Howitzer)
        225th Field Artillery Battalion (155mm Howitzer)
        477th Transportation Corps Amphibious Truck Company (Colored)
    Prov AAA Group (US Army)
        751st AAA Gun Battalion (90mm) (-)
        864th AAA Automatic Weapons Battalion (40mm/.50cal) (-)
1st Battalion, 2nd Marines (+) (Eastern Landing Group)

2nd Marine Division
Combat Team 2
    2nd Marines (+) (- 1st Battalion)
    Company A (-), 1st Battalion [engineer], 18th Marines
    Company E (-), 2nd Medical Battalion
    1st Battalion, 29th Infantry (+)
Combat Team 6
    6th Marines (+)
    2nd Amphibian Tractor Battalion [LVT(2)/(4)]
    Company B, 1st Battalion [engineer], 18th Marines
    Company D, 2nd Medical Battalion
    Company A (+), 2nd Tank Battalion [M4A2]
    2nd Prov Rocket Detachment (-)
Combat Team 8
    8th Marines (+)
    715th Amphibian Tractor Battalion [LVT(2)/(4)] (US Army)
    Company C, 1st Battalion [engineer], 18th Marines
    Company C, 2nd Medical Battalion
    Company A (+), 2nd Tank Battalion [M4A2]
    Detachment, 2nd Prov Rocket Detachment
Division Artillery
    10th Marines (artillery)
    2nd 155mm Howitzer Battalion, VAC
    Marine Observation Squadron 2
    2nd Armored Amphibian Tractor Battalion (LVT[A]4)
Support Group
    HQ&S Company, 18th Marines (engineer)
    HQ Company, 1st Battalion [engineer], 18th Marines
    HQ Battalion, 2nd MarDiv
    2nd Medical Battalion (-)
    2nd Tank Battalion (-)
    2nd Service Battalion (-)
    5th Amphibian Tractor Battalion (-) [LVT(4)]
    18th NC Battalion
    2nd Joint Assault Signal Company (-)

4th Marine Division
Regimental Landing Team 23
    23rd Marines (+)
    10th Amphibian Tractor Battalion (-) [LVT(2)]
        Company C, 11th Amphibian Tractor Battalion [LVT(2)]
        Company B, 534th Amphibian Tractor Battalion (+) [LVT(2)/(4)] (US Army)

    708th Amphibian Tank Battalion (-) [LVT(A)1/(A)4] (US Army)
    121st NC Battalion (+)
    Company C, 1st Battalion [engineer], 20th Marines
    Company C, 4th Medical Battalion
    Company C, 4th MT Battalion
    Company B, 4th Tank Battalion [M4A2]
    Company C, 4th Tank Battalion [M4A2]
    Company D (Flamethrower) (-), 4th Tank Battalion [M3A1/M5A1]
    311th Transportation Corps Port Company (Colored) (US Army)
Regimental Landing Team 25
    25th Marines (+)
    773rd Amphibian Tractor Battalion (US Army) [LVT(2)]
        Company C, 534th Amphibian Tractor Battalion (US Army) (-) [LVT(2)/(4)]
    Company C, 708th Amphibian Tank Battalion (US Army) [LVT(A)1]
    Company D, 708th Amphibian Tank Battalion (US Army) [LVT(A)1]
    2nd Battalion [pioneer], 20th Marines
    Company A, 1st Battalion [engineer], 20th Marines
    Company A, 4th Medical Battalion
    Company A, 4th MT Battalion
    Company A, 4th Tank Battalion [M4A2]
    539th Transportation Corps Port Company (Colored) (US Army)
Regimental Landing Team 24 [Division Reserve]
    24th Marines (+)
    Company B, 1st Battalion [engineer], 20th Marines
    Company B, 4th Medical Battalion
    Company B, 4th MT Battalion
    539th Transportation Corps Port Company (Colored) (US Army)
Division Artillery
    14th Marines (artillery)
    4th 105mm Artillery Battalion, VAC
    2nd Marine Amphibian Truck Company
Division Engineers
    20th Marines [engineer] (-)
    HQ, 7th Field Depot
Support Group
    HQ Battalion (-), 4th MarDiv
    4th Medical Battalion (-)
    4th MT Battalion (-)
    4th Tank Battalion (-)
    4th Service Battalion (-)
    534th Amphibian Tractor Battalion (-) (US Army)
    4th Reconnaissance Company
    Marine Observation Squadron 4
    1st Joint Assault Signal Company (-)
    1st Prov Rocket Detachment

27th Infantry Division
HQ and HQ Company, 27th InfDiv
Division Troops
    102 Engineer Combat Battalion (-)
    102nd Medical Battalion (-)
    27th Cavalry Reconnaissance Troop
Division Special Troops
    HQ, Special Troops, 27th InfDiv
    27th Signal Company
    727th Ordnance Light Maintenance Company (-)
    27th Quartermaster Company
    Prov Amphibian Truck Company, 27th InfDiv [DUKW]
    27th Counter Intelligence Corps Detachment
    27th Military Police Platoon (-)
Division Artillery
    HQ and HQ Battery, 27th InfDiv Artillery
    106th Field Artillery Battalion (155mm Howitzer)
105th Regimental Combat Team
    105th Infantry Regiment
    249th Field Artillery Battalion (105mm Howitzer)
    34th Engineer Combat Battalion [shore party]
    Company A, 102nd Engineer Combat Battalion
    Company D, 762nd Prov Tank Battalion [M5A1]
    Company A, 102nd Medical Battalion
106th Regimental Combat Team
    106th Infantry Regiment
    104th Field Artillery Battalion (105mm Howitzer)
    1341st Engineer Combat Battalion [shore party]
    Company B, 102nd Engineer Combat Battalion
    Company C, 102nd Medical Battalion
165th Regimental Combat Team
    105th Field Artillery Battalion (105mm Howitzer)
    152nd Engineer Combat Battalion [shore party]
    Company C, 102nd Engineer Combat Battalion
    Company D, 766th Tank Battalion [M5A1]
    Company B, 102nd Medical Battalion
Attachments
    1165th Engineer Combat Group [shore party]
    762nd Prov Tank Battalion (-)
    Company C, 88th Chemical Battalion (Motorized) [4.2-in mortar]
    38th Medical Field Hospital
    98th Medical Portable Surgical Hospital
    295th Joint Assault Signal Company (-)
    604th Quartermaster Graves Registration Company (-)
    95th Ordnance Bomb Disposal Squadron (USAAF)

TINIAN

Northern Troops and Landing Force (TG 56.1)/VAC
VAC HQ&S Battalion (-)
VAC Amphibious Reconnaissance Battalion
Companies D and E, VAC Medical Battalion
VAC MT Company (-)
VAC Signal Battalion (-)
VAC Prov Engineer Group
    18th and 121st NC Battalions
    34th Engineer Combat Battalion (US Army)
HQ, NTLF Shore Party
17th AAA Battalion (Island Command, Tinian)
7th Field Depot (+) (-)
3rd Marine Ammunition Company (-)
18th, 19th, and 20th Marine Depot Companies
31st and 38th Medical Field Hospitals (US Army)
96th, 97th, and 98th Medical Portable Surgical Hospitals (US Army)
477th Transportation Corps Amphibian Truck Company (-)

XXIV CORPS ARTILLERY
HQ and HQ Battery, XXIV Corps Artillery (US Army)
Groupment A [105mm]
    HQ&S Battery, 10th Marines
    3rd and 4th Battalions, 10th Marines
    3rd and 4th Battalions, 14th Marines
    4th 105mm Artillery Battalion, VAC
Groupment B [105mm]
    HQ and HQ Battery, 27th InfDiv Artillery (US Army)
    104th, 105th, and 249th Field Artillery Battalions (105mm Howitzer)
    Prov Amphibian Truck Company, 27th InfDiv [DUKW]
Groupment C [155mm]
    HQ and HQ Battery, 420th Field Artillery Group (US Army)
    2nd Battalion, 55th Coast Artillery Regiment (155mm Gun) (Mobile) (US Army)
    32nd Coast Artillery Gun Battalion (155mm Gun) (US Army)
    106th Field Artillery Battalion (155mm Howitzer), 27th InfDiv (US Army)
    145th and 225th Field Artillery Battalions (155mm Howitzer) (US Army)
    2nd 155mm Howitzer Battalion, VAC (USMC)

4th Marine Division
Regimental Landing Team 25
    25th Marines (+)
    708th Amphibian Tank Battalion [LVT(A)1/(A)4] (US Army)
    773rd Amphibian Tractor Battalion (+) [LVT(2)] (US Army)
    2nd Battalion [pioneer], 20th Marines [shore party]
    Company A, 4th Tank Battalion [M4A2]
    Company A, 1st Battalion [engineer], 20th Marines
Regimental Landing Team 24
    4th Marines (+)
    1st Battalion, 8th Marines
    2nd Armored Amphibian Tractor Battalion [LVT(A)4]
    2nd Amphibian Tractor Battalion (+) [LVT(2)/(4)]
    1341st Engineer Combat Battalion (US Army) [shore party]
    Company B, 4th Tank Battalion [M4A2]
    Detachment, HQ&S Battalion, 20th Marines [engineer]
    Company B, 1st Battalion [engineer], 20th Marines
Regimental Landing Team 23
    23rd Marines (+)
    10th Amphibian Tractor Battalion (-) [LVT(2)]
        Company C, 11th Amphibian Tractor Battalion [LVT(2)]
    Company C, 4th Tank Battalion [M4A2]
    Company C, 1st Battalion [engineer], 20th Marines
Division Artillery
    14th Marines (artillery) (-)
    1st and 2nd Battalions, 10th Marines [artillery]
    1st and 2nd Marine Amphibian Truck Companies
Division Engineers
    20th Marines [engineer] (-)
Support Group
    HQ Battalion, 4th MarDiv (-)
    2nd Tank Battalion [M4A2/M3A1/M5A1]
    4th Medical Battalion (-)
    4th MT Battalion (-)
    4th Tank Battalion (-)
    4th Service Battalion
    Marine Observation Squadron 4
    1st Joint Assault Signal Company (-)
    Prov HQ, Amphibian Tractors, VAC
    5th Amphibian Tractor Battalion (-) [LVT(4)]
    534th and 715th Amphibian Tractor Battalions (-) [LVT(2)/(4)] (US Army)

2nd Marine Division
Combat Team 2
    2nd Marines (+)
    Company A (-), 1st Battalion [engineer], 18th Marines
    2nd Prov Rocket Detachment (-)
Combat Team 6
    6th Marines (+)
    Company B (-), 1st Battalion [engineer], 18th Marines
Combat Team 8
    8th Marines (+) (- 1/8 until J+1)
    Company A, 1st Battalion [engineer], 18th Marines
    Collecting Section, Company C, 2nd Medical Battalion
    Detachment, 2nd Prov Rocket Detachment
Support Group
    HQ&S Company, 18th Marines [engineer]
    HQ Company, 1st Battalion [engineer], 18th Marines
    2nd Battalion [pioneer], 18th Marines (+)
    HQ Battalion, 2nd MarDiv
    2nd Medical Battalion (-)
    2nd MT Battalion (-)
    2nd Service Battalion (-)
    2nd Joint Assault Signal Company (-)

Naval Construction Battalions and UDTs
2nd Special NC Battalion
13th Special NC Battalion
18th NC Battalion (attached to 2nd MarDiv)
Detachment, 67th NC Battalion
Detachment, 92nd NC Battalion
121st NC Battalion (attached to 4th MarDiv)
302nd NC Battalion
Underwater Demolition Team 5 (supported 2nd MarDiv)
Underwater Demolition Team 6 (UDT reserve)
Underwater Demolition Team 7 (supported 4th MarDiv)

JAPANESE UNIT ORGANIZATION

JAPANESE FORCES – SAIPAN
31st Army HQ and service units
43rd Division (Northern Marianas Army Group)
    43rd Division HQ
    118th Infantry Regiment
    135th Infantry Regiment (-)[12]
    136th Infantry Regiment
    43rd Division Intendance Duty Unit[13]
    43rd Division Signal Company
    43rd Division Ordnance Company
    43rd Transport Company
    43rd Division Hospital (-)[14]

47th Independent Mixed Brigade (-)[15]
    47th IMB HQ
    316th–318th Independent Infantry Battalions
    3rd Independent Mountain Arty Regiment (-)
    47th IMB Artillery Unit
    47th IMB Engineer Unit

3rd Independent Mountain Artillery Regiment (-)[16]
9th Tank Regiment (-)[17]
III Battalion, 9th Independent Mixed Regiment
I Battalion, 18th Infantry Regiment[18]
25th AAA Regiment (-)[19]
    43rd Independent AA Company
    44th Field Machine Cannon Company
7th Independent Engineer Regiment (-)[20]
16th Shipping Engineer Regiment (-)[21]
14th and 17th Independent Artillery Mortar Battalions
4th Independent Tank Company (no tanks)
264th (-)[22] and 278th Independent Transport Companies
278th Independent Transport Company

Straggler Units
    60th Anchorage HQ
    14th Hangar Maintenance Section
    1st Intendance Security Unit
    115th Airfield Battalion
    23rd Airfield Construction Unit
    Detachments, 15th and 150th Infantry Regiments
    9th Expeditionary Unit

Central Pacific Area Fleet HQ
55th Guard Force
Detachment, 41st Guard Force
Yokosuka 1st SNLF (-)
5th Construction Department
5th Naval Stores Department
5th Communications Unit
Office of Supply and Accounts
Southeast Area Air Base
Aerological Bureau, Saipan
Tora Construction Battalion
14th Antiaircraft Maintenance Section
Air Flight U156

Japanese Forces – Tinian
50th Infantry Regiment, 29th Division
    50th Infantry Regiment HQ
    I–III Battalions
    Artillery Battalion
    Engineer Company
    Signal Company
    Supply Company
    Medical Company
    Fortification Detachment
    Antitank Platoon
I Battalion, 135th Infantry Regiment
Tank Company, 118th Infantry Regiment
Detachment, 29th Field Hospital
Platoon, 264th Independent Transport Company

1st Air Fleet HQ
56th Guard Force
82nd and 83rd AA Defense Units
116th, 233rd, and 833rd Construction Battalions
523rd Air Group service personnel
IJN air unit stragglers

Notes

10 Commanding General and Staff, Expeditionary Troops and NTLF embarked.
11 Redesignated Assault Air Warning Squadron 5 on 10 July.
12 I Battalion on Tinian.
13 Supply labor unit.
14 Element sent to Pagan on 21 May 1944.
15 315th IIB on Pagan.
16 Less II Battalion.
17 1st and 2nd Companies and half of 6th Company on Guam.
18 Parent regiment on Guam.
19 Less 3rd–5th Batteries. Remaining batteries were 1st, 2nd, and 6th.
20 2nd Company on Guam.
21 2nd Company on Guam, detachment on Pagan.
22 Platoon on Tinian.

THE BATTLEFIELD TODAY

The United Nations turned over the former Japanese Mandate to US control on 2 January 1947 as the Trust Territory of the Pacific Islands. In 1949 the UN granted the US trusteeship over the Marianas as part of the Trust Territory. Naval administration ceased on 30 June 1951. On 8 January 1978 the covenant agreement and constitution were adopted and the islands became the Commonwealth of the Northern Mariana Islands on 4 November 1986. A local governor was elected at that time. The commonwealth is in political union with the US and administered through the Department of the Interior. Saipan's town of Chalan Kanoa is now the commonwealth capital and its main seaport. The islands have no significant exports, other than a growing garment industry with most of the workers being Chinese. Most coconut, vegetable, fruit, and cattle production is consumed locally. The commonwealth's main source of income is tourism, of which about 75 percent are Japanese. Most others are Koreans, Taiwanese, and Chinese. Japanese tourism began in the 1950s when families of servicemen began visiting the islands. Today 60,000 people inhabit Saipan, Tinian, and Rota.

After the war, naval base funding and resources were channeled to Guam and the Saipan base was decommissioned on 30 June 1949. The Tinian airbases were closed after the war and much of the building debris bulldozed to the island's edges. The center of the island has overgrown with brush, high grasses, and wild sugarcane. The naval base and naval airbase were closed on 1 June 1947. Today the former Tinian Town is known as San Jose. Much of the island is leased by the US military for training and the West and North Fields' runways are still used. Little is to be found on Tinian, which is seldom visited by tourists. A small monument marks the atomic bomb loading pits and a few Japanese military buildings remain.

The Saipan American Memorial is located on the south side of Tanapag Harbor. It is part of the American Memorial Park commemorating the Americans and Chamorros who died in the fighting. Dedicated in 1994, it is inscribed with the names of over 5,000 of those killed. Unit memorial plaques are found on some of the landing beaches. Until recently there was a World War II Museum at the American Memorial Park on the north side of Garapan. This was closed when the volunteer Historical Society dissolved. The artifacts are under the care of the US National Parks Service pending reopening. A virtual museum can be found at *www.nps.gov/amme/wwii_museum/ amp_ww2_museum.html*

The Commonwealth of the Northern Mariana Islands Museum of History and Culture is located in an old Japanese hospital on the south side of Garapan. Japanese memorials exist at the island's north end on what are known as Banzai and Suicide Cliffs where Japanese soldiers and civilians threw themselves off. Rusting weapons and equipment can still be found in the hills and a great deal of equipment lies below the waters in Tanapag Harbor and off the landing beaches. The waters provide excellent scuba diving. War relics are protected by law and cannot be removed. Before the law was enacted tons of equipment was salvaged and sold for scrap. Pillboxes and gun emplacements still survive in the hills. The last Japanese CP is located in the restored Banadero Cave near Marpi Point. Rusting tank hulks, vehicles, and weapons are displayed there. A word of caution to tourists; many World War II-era place names have been replaced by Chamorro or Spanish names on maps and signs.

BIBLIOGRAPHY

Chapin, Capt John C., *Breaching the Marianas: The Battle for Saipan.* Washington Navy Yard: History and Museums Division, Marine Corps Historical Center, 1994.

Craven, Wesley F. and Cate, James L., *The Army Air Forces in World War II: The Pacific: Guadalcanal to Saipan, August 1942 to July 1944, Vol. 4.* Chicago: University of Chicago Press, 1950.

Crowl, Philip A., *United States Army in World War II: Campaign in the Marianas.* Washington: US Government Printing Office, 1960.

Fuller, Richard., *Shokan – Hirohito's Samurai: Leaders of the Japanese Armed Forces 1926–1945.* London: Arms and Armour Press, 1992.

Gailey, Harry A., *Howlin Mad vs. the Army: Conflict in Command, Saipan, 1944.* Novato: Presidio Press, 1986.

Gugeler, Russell A., *Army Amphibian Tractor and Tank Battalions in the Battle of Saipan 15 June–19 July 1944.* US Army Center of Military History, 1945. Available on-line at: http://www.army.mil/cmh-pg/documents/wwii/amsai/amsai.htm

Harwood, Richard., *A Close Encounter: The Marine Landing on Tinian.* Washington Navy Yard: History and Museums Division, Marine Corps Historical Center, 1994.

Hoffman, Maj Carl W., *Saipan: The Beginning of the End.* Washington: Historical Division, US Marine Corps, 1950. (Battery Press reprint available)

Hoffman, Maj Carl W., *The Seizure of Tinian.* Washington: HQ Marine Corps, 1951. (Battery Press reprint available)

Hoyt, Edwin P., *To the Marianas: War in the Central Pacific 1944.* New York: Van Norstrad Reinhold, 1990.

Johnston, Richard W., *Follow Me! The Story of the Second Marine Division in World War II.* New York: Random House, 1948. (Battery Press reprint available)

Jones, Don., *Oba, the Last Samurai: Saipan, 1944–45.* Novato, CA: Presidio Press, 1986.

Morison, Samuel E., *History of US Navy Operations in World War II: New Guinea and the Marianas, March 1944–August 1944, Vol. VIII.* Boston: Little, Brown and Company, 1958.

Petty, Bruce M., *Saipan: Oral Histories of the Pacific War.* Jefferson, NC: McFarland and Company, 2002.

Proehl, Carl W., *The Fourth Marine Division in World War II.* Washington, DC: Infantry Journal Press, Inc., 1946. (Battery Press reprint available)

Rottman, Gordon L., *US Marine Corps Order of Battle: Ground and Air Units in the Pacific War, 1939-1940.* Westport, CT: Greenwood Publishing, 2002.

Rottman, Gordon L., *World War II Pacific Island Guide: A Geo-Military Study.* Westport, CT: Greenwood Publishing, 2002.

Shaw, Henry I. Jr., Nalty, Bernard C., and Turnbladh, Edwin T., *History of US Marine Corps Operations in World War II: Central Pacific Drive, Vol. III.* Washington: US Government Printing Office, 1966.

Stanton, Shelby L., *Order of Battle, U.S. Army, World War II.* Novato, CA: Presidio Press, 1984.

Tillman, Barrett., *Carrier Battle in the Philippine Sea: The Marianas Turkey Shoot.* St Paul, MN: Phalanx, 1994.

INDEX